THE TEACHINGS OF THE STOICS

THE TEACHINGS OF THE STOICS

DAILY INSPIRATIONS FOR FINDING INNER PEACE

MICHAEL MOORE

This edition published in 2025 by Arcturus Publishing Limited
26/27 Bickels Yard, 151–153 Bermondsey Street,
London SE1 3HA

Copyright © Arcturus Holdings Limited

All rights reserved. No part of this publication may be reproduced, stored in a retrieval system, or transmitted, in any form or by any means, electronic, mechanical, photocopying, recording or otherwise, without prior written permission in accordance with the provisions of the Copyright Act 1956 (as amended). Any person or persons who do any unauthorised act in relation to this publication may be liable to criminal prosecution and civil claims for damages.

AD012793US

Printed in China

CONTENTS

INTRODUCTION 7

CHAPTER 1 Zeno 13

CHAPTER 2 Cleanthes and Chrysippus 23

CHAPTER 3 Virtue 33

CHAPTER 4 Nature 43

CHAPTER 5 The Passions 52

CHAPTER 6 The Gods 62

CHAPTER 7 Politics 72

CHAPTER 8 Seneca 81

CHAPTER 9 Marcus Aurelius 90

CHAPTER 10 Epictetus 99

CHAPTER 11 Impression 109

CHAPTER 12 Neo-Stoicism 118

INDEX 126

INTRODUCTION

Athens is known as the birthplace of philosophy. It is the city of Socrates, Plato, and Aristotle and the schools of thought they established. Plato instructed his pupils at the Academy, Aristotle at the Lyceum. Following the deaths of these giants, more schools were established, with their own masters, programs, influences, and trajectories. Among these were Stoicism, instituted by Zeno of Citium, located at the so-called Painted Porch in the city's main square, the Agora, and Epicureanism, founded by Epicurus and situated just outside Athens at what became known as the Garden. This context is important to understand, as it shows how Stoicism emerged alongside and in competition with other schools for students and for intellectual legitimacy.

It was in the cut and thrust of philosophical disputation with rival modes of thought that Stoic beliefs came to be defined. While the Epicureans, for example, argued that the aim of all living creatures, human and animal, was the pursuit of pleasure and the avoidance of pain, the Stoics maintained instead that there was no overarching mode of behavior that could be applied to all creatures equally. To the Stoic mind, each creature sought to fulfill its individual nature according to the particular circumstances in which it found itself in any given moment. Similarly, disagreements with the heirs of Plato's Academy over the nature of knowledge helped the Stoics to clarify and fortify their philosophical position on that subject and other matters. So it was that, through the scrum of analytical debate, the main tenets of Stoicism were formed.

The battles between the Stoics and other philosophical schools were not merely scholarly disagreements over academic minutiae. The Painted Porch in the Agora under which its

The Stoa Poikile, *or Painted Porch, in Athens, where the Stoics fought their intellectual battles.*

adherents met was part of the Stoa, the portico from which the Stoics took their name. By choosing such a central location to gather, the school was making a very explicit and public pitch to gain new converts to its philosophy. Stoicism's success in its skirmishes with other schools conferred legitimacy on both what was being taught and on its teachers. It should also be mentioned that at least the first two founders of the school, Zeno and Cleanthes, appeared to be dependent on public contributions for their livelihood. They had to make compelling, not to mention persuasive, arguments in order to attract potential (and possibly paying) students, serious or casual.

Stoicism in a way is a very easy philosophy to study, for it divides philosophy neatly into three parts: Ethics, Logic, and Physics. It can be viewed as a system, a rigorous and clear exposition with beliefs and practices. This was and continues to be part of its appeal, a practical philosophy which can be divided into easy parts for immediate application. Its history is fascinating and even those parts of its doctrines which hold no practical value still hold interest even when they have no direct influence on our ethical life.

In this book we look at the major figures in the history of Stoicism. This includes the three first heads of the Stoa, Zeno, Cleanthes, and Chrysippus, and the three most significant popularizers of Stoicism throughout the ages, Seneca, Epictetus and Marcus Aurelius. The three founders are often the most authoritative voices within the tradition of Stoicism in antiquity, with Zeno possessing a unique and almost religious claim to infallibility among the Stoics that followed. They created the Stoic world and populated it with a depth of thought and coherency that was to last for centuries. But the three popularizers also did much to shape Stoicism as we think of it today, with their focus on moral development. Seneca, Epictetus, and Marcus Aurelius share many themes in common, but they did not lay out their beliefs in a "system." Instead—as many Stoics do today—they adapted the teachings of the founders to their own circumstances and wrote powerfully and persuasively on subjects such as the call to virtue, the autonomy of our choices, our indifference to irrelevant matters, the turn to inward progress, the appreciation of our common nature with all humans, and the downplaying of reputation and human opinion.

For Marcus Aurelius and Epictetus I have paraphrased the books or chapters within their most famous works, the *Meditations* and *Encheiridion*, respectively. This complements the works themselves, which are conversational, informal, and striking in their brevity and insight. For Seneca, whose output is much broader, I have centered several important themes found throughout his moral essays to give a representative, if not complete, view of his philosophy. If it is at all possible, these authors should also be read as primary texts.

In its structure, as well as looking at the main figures in Stoicism, this book addresses all of the philosophy's key topics, chapter by chapter. These include virtue, nature, passions, the gods, politics, impression, and a concluding chapter on the present-day phenomenon of Neo-Stoicism. These chapters contain the most important, and often the most controversial, doctrines of Stoicism, such as the role of the passions and how the school's theory of knowledge is bound up with its concept of "presentation."

Marcus Aurelius, Roman emperor and Stoic philosopher. Like all the Stoics, he adapted his beliefs to the circumstances in which he lived and made persuasive arguments on how to live in his Meditations.

What I hope to communicate in these chapters is that Stoicism was a complex system integrating many different ideas into a unified philosophy. So while individual Stoics sometimes disagreed on the details, their commitment to the fundamentals of Stoicism was unquestioned. With that said, although the chapters can be read individually, it is better to read them in order. This is because there is a logic and a rhythm to the way Stoicism is set out. The peculiar nature of Stoic physics, seen in the chapter on Nature, helps to explain the Stoic relationship with the divine. Likewise, the emphasis on Virtue in Chapter 3 lays the groundwork for why the passions are to be eliminated in Chapter 5.

This collection includes a series of cards to help incorporate Stoic practices of thinking and behaviour into your own life. Use them any time you have a few minutes to contemplate their meaning and be receptive to their impact. First take a card, read the front and back, and imagine how you can bring the card to bear on your own life. Next you will take a small step in development by acting according to Stoic advice. "Patience with the limitations of others," or s"pending your time on only important activities" are easy to acknowledge, but what you want is to live and practice these ideas. Stick with the same card for a few days in a row, set it aside and re-evaluate a few weeks or even months later. If you are giving it due attention, you will certainly improve. Now the goal will be to keep this going with persistent attention until these practices become engrained habits.

You will find much to admire and much to puzzle over in this ancient philosophy. The contents of this book will either entertain or enlighten you. I hope that at most times it will accomplish both.

CHAPTER 1
Zeno

Zeno of Citium (*c*.334 BC–*c*.262 BC) founded Stoicism. As noted in the Introduction, Stoicism did not develop in a philosophical vacuum. Zeno was known to have listened to lectures by Xenocrates and Polemo, the third and fourth principals respectively of Plato's Academy, as well as the thinker Stilpo, who belonged to the so-called Megarian school. On a more esoteric level, Zeno was also known to have visited the Oracle at Delphi to seek its answers on how to live the best life. The answer it gave was that he had to become the same color as the dead. Zeno understood this as an instruction to read dead authors. Already in these early biographical anecdotes we can see that Zeno was reacting to and being formed by his historical predecessors.

Socrates was of course an influence, as he has been on all philosophers. Zeno was in a bookshop one day reading about the excellence of Socrates in a work by Xenophon when he exclaimed aloud that he wished to learn from someone like him. "Follow this one," the bookshop owner said, pointing to the Cynic philosopher Crates, who happened to be passing by. Taking the bookseller's advice, Zeno became a student of Crates for a while. It was from this robust experience with a variety of philosophies and personal encounters with different philosophers—Academic, Cynic, Megarian, Socratic—that Zeno began to forge his unique philosophical school.

PHILOSOPHICAL SCHOOLS ZENO ENGAGED WITH

School	Founder or influence
Peripatetic	Aristotle
Academic	Plato
Megarian	A pupil of Socrates

THE "STOA" AND STOICISM

The origin of the term Stoic comes from the location where the Stoics would meet. In this respect it was similar to the Academy, which took its name from the grove dedicated to the hero Akademus where Plato taught his first followers. When Plato's former pupil Aristotle established his own school, known as the Lyceum, he continued this tradition and named it after the gymnasium where it was based (whose name in turn came from it being dedicated to Apollo in the guise of the wolf-god, Lyceus). Situated on the north side of the Agora, the main public square in Athens, the Stoa was the portico or colonnade in which the early Stoics practiced their philosophical discourses. Because it was decorated with works by the artist Polygnotus, this colonnade was often referred to as the *Stoa Poikile*, or Painted Porch. It was here that Zeno began giving philosophical discourses sometime around 300 BC and soon began to gather an impressive audience for himself. Despite his success in drawing a crowd, there exist a number of curious testimonies indicating that Zeno was ambivalent about his popularity. He would sit on the end of a couch to avoid human contact, it was claimed, or ask for money so that people would be less willing to approach him. He was even said to have installed a small fence in the porch, to ensure that his listeners could not come too close.

Perhaps it was this rather antisocial attitude that explains the many witticisms of his we have on record, which are almost exclusively biting remarks delivered in social contexts.

When a slave caught pilfering pleaded that it was his fate to steal, Zeno told him that it was his fate to be beaten as well.

NEW PHILOSOPHY

One reputation, or charge, that Zeno acquired from his earliest public career was that he had simply stolen all of his philosophy from others. While the wealth and pervasiveness of philosophical ideas in circulation during Zeno's day offered the chance for an unprecedented training in this emerging field of knowledge, it also gave critics an easy opportunity to claim

Zeno of Citium.

Zeno had nothing original to say. Polemo even made this charge explicit, interrupting his own lecture attended by Zeno, to claim that Zeno attended only to snatch his words and turn them into something Phoenician. (Zeno was from Citium, a Phoenician colony.)

THE THREE DIVISIONS OF PHILOSOPHY

Stoic philosophy is divided into three parts—Ethics, Logic, and Physics—a distinction supposedly outlined by Zeno in his book *On the Word* (only fragments of his works survive, so much of what we know about Zeno's thought is based on tradition or on the testimonies of his followers and, in some cases, critics). When describing these divisions, the Stoics often used analogies from nature. Philosophy was like an animal body, they said, with ethics as the flesh, logic the sinews and bones, and physics the soul. Or perhaps it was an egg, with the shell as logic, the white as ethics, and the yolk as physics. For some Stoics, their philosophical system was a garden where logic was its fence, ethics its crop, and physics its soil.

There are several broad points to be taken from Zeno's tripartite division. As the analogies mentioned above show quite vividly, it impresses upon us the indivisibility of those three divisions. Yes these are three distinct fields within a philosophy, but they can never be entirely separated from each other, either in thought or in action. If philosophy is like a garden, then it is within the boundaries and structures of logic that philosophy can truly grow, just as a garden needs to have a structure to keep out pests, prevent weeds, and be productive. The crop is indeed the most important element in the garden. It is what we cultivate a garden for, so that we can have fruits and vegetables. But the crop is dependent not only on the structure of the fence, symbolically the stand-in for logic, but on the nutriment from the earth and plants, symbolically the stand-in for physics. Two different truths are emphasized simultaneously. Ethics, logic, and physics are each dependent on the other, and, at the same time, no single one of these branches makes sense without the other. This should give a good indication of the seriousness with which Zeno treated philosophy. Everything was understood to interact in a certain way, and no part of knowledge could be taken for granted. Later Stoics subdivided these parts of philosophy even further, and they disagreed on which part should be taught first: some saying ethics; others physics. But this basic division into three remained.

PHYSICS

What, then, is physics according to the Stoic conception? The word comes from *physis*, the Greek term for nature, so in this respect the physics of Stoicism is concerned with all things that exist. For the Stoics—and many other Greek thinkers in antiquity—nature was divided into the four elements of fire, air, earth, and water. But this does not tell the whole story. Even if we want to assert that a rose bush is made of some combination of the four elements (or atoms, as our contemporary science would affirm) the bush also possesses flowers, stems, thorns, leaves, and so forth. Even scent is a part of the rose bush.

So, depending on the vantage point from which we divide up the world, the "physics" we use to describe it will change. The Stoics were similar to us in this way. The most radical of their physical doctrines is that only bodies exist. This is a commitment to materialism, the belief that there are only physical or material objects. The soul, in their view, was not non-existent; it was something physical that could not be seen. A position declaring that everything is matter is not as simple as it seems, however. For the Stoics also said that there is a level of something that can be called secondary existence. They put forth four of these exceptions to the general idea that everything that exists is made of matter: time, place, void, and the "sayable."

To understand the distinction between what really exists, as something corporeal, and what does not, simply because it is not corporeal, we need to look at what is distinctive about bodies. The idea is quite simple. According to Stoicism, in order to affect something else, or to be affected, a thing has to be material. A fish can move the water, only because it and the wave it pushes away from itself with its fin are physical. A splinter is real because it can cause a deep pain in your skin, since both the splinter and skin are material objects. The Stoic contends that anything that is truly immaterial has no power to affect a material thing or can in turn be affected by it. Putting aside "sayables" for a moment, it also seems reasonable to apply this same principle to time, place, and void. These three things involve circumstances in which truly existing things, such as a person, can exist and do the sort of things that physical things do, like stand, or push, or watch a movie. Time, place, and void are said to "subsist" in this way. They possess a limited and derivative form of existence compared to physical things. One could say that they are not real things in themselves but depend on other things for their existence. To "subsist" means "to stand under" and it is probably best to conceive of them in this way. When you think of time or place, it is very difficult to think of them as capable of bringing about an effect or being affected. When, for example, you think of grass or a house, both exist within a place and a time, and they are physical things existing within place and time, but they are not quite identical to place and time either.

Now if we return to the analysis of a sayable, this is what lies behind something uttered or written, and is intimately associated with language, but not to be identified with it. For example, in English, Greek, and Latin respectively, the word for "tree" is tree, *dendron*, and *arbor*. Yet the sayable for all three of these words—the concept of a tree—is the same. A tree exists as a physical thing, but so too does the immaterial idea of the tree, its sayable.

Sayables

The word for tree
English: tree
Latin: arbor
Greek: dendron

The actual object

The "sayable": The idea of the object

ETHICS

Stoic Ethics has several interacting elements, all of which are important. Following the tradition of Plato and Aristotle, Zeno too sought the path of the happy life. For the Stoics, this pathway could only be found through virtue. In the Stoic belief system, a person can lack every other grace and good in life, but if they are in possession of virtue they are nevertheless deemed happy. This single-minded devotion to virtue is also described as living in accordance with reason and nature. Man's nature is essentially rational, and to live in accordance with this nature is to be rational. To be truly rational is to pursue and possess virtue. As it turns out, the possession of virtue is quite a task and is rarely, if ever, attained. Only a Stoic "sage," an exemplar of rare quality, can achieve this level of moral perfection.

LOGIC

Along with physics, the logic of Stoicism is also neglected in comparison to ethics. In the various biographical fragments we have of the life of Zeno, it tells us that he had a keen interest in this area of philosophy. Logic comes from the Greek word *logos*, a term which denotes both "reason" and "language." So logic concerns rhetoric, logic, language, and grammar. One area of logic we have already touched on is the sayables. But the Stoics were also interested in taxonomies of language, the meaning and the logical relationships among different premises. As we will see, Stoicism became more sophisticated as it developed. This won it more followers, but earned it enemies, too—most notably the Epicureans—and the battlefield they engaged on often concerned the exact meanings of their beliefs. In the context of debate, philosophical precision requires the close analysis of language, both to defend and articulate Stoic positions, but also to attack the vulnerabilities in the arguments of others.

Zeno loomed as an authoritative figure in Stoicism for decades, supplying its basic framework but leaving plenty of room for his successors to fill in the gaps, and even bicker between themselves. Though most of his writings are lost, his ideas survive in the work of his successors who had the freedom to expand upon his philosophy but not build something entirely new.

Epicurus and his followers fiercely contested the ideas of the Stoics.

CHAPTER 2
Cleanthes and Chrysippus

In this chapter we will look at the two heads of the Stoa after Zeno, Cleanthes (331 BC–232 BC) and Chrysippus (280 BC–206 BC). They are taken together because their unique personalities give us a further sense of how the philosophical doctrine of the Stoa evolved. Though Cleanthes followed Zeno, we will find that it is in Chrysippus that Stoicism really gets its footing for the centuries to come. Given this imbalance in importance, it is not surprising that we have much less information about Cleanthes than Chrysippus.

CLEANTHES

The second person in charge of the Stoa after Zeno was Cleanthes. From the sources we have, we do not know how the heads of the Stoic school were chosen, nor for that matter if they were chosen, or anointed, or voted for. It is thought that they served in their role for life once selected. Cleanthes, from the provincial town of Assos in modern-day western Turkey, does not fit the aristocratic stereotype many people have of Greek philosophers. When he arrived in Athens to study under Zeno, he was a boxer. His lack of money led him to take on work gardening at night to sustain his philosophical studies during the day, using some of the meager funds he earned to pay for his tuition. Unable to afford expensive paper, he wrote his notes on Zeno's lectures on oyster shells and animal bones.

Unlike some of his quick-witted colleagues, Cleanthes was at first mocked—he was given the nickname "the ass"—and then renowned for his slow and steady character. It was this quality, as well as his capacity for hard work, that led to Cleanthes becoming Zeno's successor after almost 20 years as his disciple. He then served as the head of the Stoic school for 32 years. Cleanthes wrote dozens of works, of which only fragments survive, and is said to have starved himself to death aged 99: having been told to fast to help cure a painful ulcer, he decided not to eat again once he had recovered, claiming that he was too far down the road to death to turn back.

Cleanthes.

CHRYSIPPUS

By all accounts a formidable philosopher, Chrysippus is regarded as the "second founder" of Stoicism for his many contributions to its logic and system. So indebted is Stoic thought to his developments that it is said that without Chrysippus the school would not have survived.

Like his predecessor Cleanthes, Chrysippus was an athlete. He was a long distance runner rather than a boxer, but clearly for the early Stoics the idea of mastery over the body was seen as a counterpart to understanding the rigors of philosophy.

Chrysippus.

Unlike Cleanthes, Chrysippus was quite gifted intellectually. An insightful anecdote is told that he grew impatient with the lectures of Cleanthes and asked his master to tell him what the Stoic positions were on philosophical issues so that he could develop the arguments to support them on his own. He was even more productive than Cleanthes, writing more than 700 books, but, as with many of the philosophers of antiquity, most of his output has been lost.

SUCCESSION DISPUTES

As was implied at the beginning of this chapter, Cleanthes and Chrysippus, standing at the headwaters of Stoicism, were necessarily influential. But this does not mean their tenures were in full agreement. One of the difficulties faced in the aftermath of Zeno's death was to determine what his opinion would have been on unresolved or new philosophical problems that emerged after his demise. One example was the dispute over "impressions," a Stoic technical term we will look at in Chapter 11. For simplicity's sake, an impression can be something that we perceive, say a man walking or a red apple sitting on a table. Cleanthes thought that these impressions were literal imprints in our physical souls, like little images sitting inside the warehouse of our memory. Chrysippus, while not disputing the existence of these impressions, thought they were only metaphorical images. There were other disputes like this, all of which referred back to Zeno and granted a level of authority to his writing. The school, although it faced disagreement among the first two heads after the founder, at least had settled on this: that Zeno and Stoicism cannot be separated. To follow Stoicism is to follow Zeno.

At any rate, the uncertain state that Zeno left his school in provided an opportunity for a more systematic approach to Stoicism. If Stoicism were to grow as a philosophical school, as in fact it did, it would have to become more rigorous. It was helped in this by the attacks it faced from Plato's Academy. By the time Chrysippus was head of the Stoa, the Academy had turned toward skeptical arguments about knowledge, many of which were aimed directly at the Stoics' teachings on this subject. In defending themselves against intellectual assault, the Stoics were forced to define their positions. Not that all of these onslaughts came from external sources, especially in regard to Chrysippus. He was also attacked by later Stoics, which is an indication both of his influence and a sign that perhaps his contributions to Stoicism were closer to innovations than developments adhering to Zeno's original intent. By Epictetus's time (AD 50–135), we read several times in his *Discourses* that the virtue and wisdom found in Stoicism are not to be identified with merely reading some of Chrysippus's works. Epictetus does not seem to be criticizing so much as admonishing his listeners to avoid relying exclusively on Chrysippus. These reports of resistance to Chrysippus give good evidence of his popularity, perhaps even his overpopularity, which had to be aligned with the fact that Zeno, not Chrysippus, was the authoritative founder of Stoicism.

ARGUMENTATION

Some of the fragments of Chrysippus's work that survive give us a good indication of the philosopher's interests. These dense little arguments play on some ambiguity in the use of words. Take the following argument: Whoever divulges the sacred mysteries to the uninitiated is impious; the priest divulges sacred mysteries to the uninitiated, therefore the priest is impious. He also constructed absurd arguments.

It is easy to dismiss these arguments as trivial word games, but in them one can see the nose for logical precision for which Stoicism came to be known. One can even see, in the argument about the wagon "going through your mouth," a distinction between the meaning of a word and the oral and written symbol which stands in for that thing.

CHRYSIPPUS'S LOGIC

For Chrysippus, Logic was the "practice of right reason." Despite the obviousness of the definition, the idea strikes at the practicality of logic. Logic is not merely some abstraction, akin to a mathematical game, nor a word chopping activity. It was fundamentally necessary to our getting along in the world. This is because we have to understand what we and others are really saying, but also because we have to test what we say to ensure it is true. Chrysippus was not slinging syllogisms for their own sake; the primary aim of logic for him and other Stoics was to discover what things are good and which bad.

THE SOUL

As in all Greek philosophy, the soul is the seat of thinking. In Chrysippus's Stoicism we see an emphasis on the unity of the soul. This is partly a rejection of the view of the soul, especially in Plato, but also suggested by Aristotle, that the soul has many parts.

This is not to say that Chrysippus has wholly done away with dividing the soul up in some way. What he really objects to is a separation between the different powers or faculties of the soul. It is understood to be a rational whole and is in fact inseparable from the body, since both are made of matter. In one fragment we have, Chrysippus says that the different sense perceptions are like branches of a tree. The tree in this metaphor is the ruling part of the soul, termed the *hegemonikon*, which is further compared to a king. This "king" passes judgments on what the sense perceptions deliver to it, making a determination of what object is before it through inference. The *hegemonikon* also remembers and uses foresight to determine what will happen in the future. In a vivid illustration of Chrysippus's commitment to materialism, he explains that individual perceptions are conducted through breath or air that is moved internally in the body.

CHRYSIPPEAN PHYSICS

Physics is the nature—and the study of the nature—of the things that exist. Chrysippus posited a fundamental division between everything in the universe: active and passive. In Zeno's phrasing, there is that which acts and that which is acted upon. The passive element is what we would call matter. The active element is breath, or *pneuma*, which is also identified with Zeus. Pneuma is the mixture of fire and air, with the fire component referring to the fact that breath is warm.

The difference between matter and pneuma could not be starker. Matter is entirely inert and incapable of any characterization without the guiding power of pneuma. Pneuma is a creative, unifying, and preserving force throughout the universe—thus its identification with Zeus. This dynamic feature of pneuma is not limited to the general structure of the universe. It is this same pneuma that permeates the body of a human to give life and rationality.

CHRYSIPPUS AND ETHICS

As we will see later in our exploration of Stoic ethics, the leadership of Chrysippus affirmed the basic moral principles laid down by Zeno and then Cleanthes, and which in turn had been highly influenced by Plato and Aristotle and their schools. Through this tradition, there was an accepted position that the goal of human life was happiness, which the Greeks termed *eudaimonia*. Since happiness was desirable, there was considerable interest in how it was attained.

Nature loomed large in Chrysippus's explanation of how people live and ought to live. To illustrate this, a distinction was made between animals and humans. When an animal is born it immediately begins to seek the self-preservation of its body. This is innate and untaught, and it ensures that all animals are instinctively drawn toward living out their natures. In the case of man, this instinct can be thwarted. As a rational creature, man also has the opportunity to turn to the irrational. One important contrast this is meant to bring out is that organisms are not primarily motivated by pleasure and pain, a position the Stoics were to contest strenuously in their disagreement with the Epicureans. A memorable example of Chrysippus's idea was later given by Seneca. He said that a turtle when turned upon its back will seek to right itself. Seneca's emphasis is that a turtle is not really seeking pleasure, nor even avoiding pain, but it is seeking the position where it can live as a turtle. This, of course, involves its body, which can only live on the ground with its carapace up and its four feet on the ground. The suggestion is that humans too have a correct role, a rational one, to live out in the world they find themselves in.

CHAPTER 3

Virtue

Virtue is an important part of any philosophy, for it concerns the way we do and should act, and so involves itself deeply with the field of ethics. But particularly in the case of Stoicism, virtue takes center stage and becomes a singular focus of human life. The Greek term we translate as "virtue" is *arete*, a word with a wide application to anything which is excellent in its kind.

The importance of virtue cannot be separated from its role in the attainment of happiness. For the Stoics, even to say that virtue has a role in happiness is a grand understatement. Virtue is almost identical to happiness. Once virtue is attained, then happiness comes into being. This immediately gives us a sense of the seriousness which Stoicism gives to the identification and cultivation of different virtues, even where it opens them up to criticism. So steadfast was this commitment to virtue that the

Stoics infamously said that even on the torture rack a virtuous man would be happy. Whether you agree with the Stoic position or their critics, one thing that is made clear by this extreme position is that if the attainment of virtue is happiness, then virtue cannot merely be an idea or emotion or else it would be unable to persist during torture.

THE HUMAN POSITION

In the most general terms, the actions which make up virtue are things "in our power." In Epictetus's great work, the *Discourses*, he begins by discussing the things up to us and the things not up to us. Virtue and vice, and choosing virtue or vice, are the most important things in our power. Many things are not in our power: our place of birth, upbringing, our physical looks, the diseases we suffer from. These are not to be the focus of our attention. We can control only what is controllable by a human.

THE CENTRALITY OF VIRTUE

Virtue takes up such importance in Stoicism that in a very real sense it crowds out all other concerns. Everything else in life is subordinate to the aim of attaining virtue. In this way it is independent, and due to its unique character no appeals are made to pursue virtue apart from virtue itself. Virtue is to be valued for its own sake: other things are measured by their virtue; virtue has no higher value by which it can be measured.

THE NATURE OF VIRTUE

The Stoics, like most ancient Greeks, philosophical or not, readily embraced the cardinal virtues: wisdom, temperance, courage, and justice. Other Stoics added more virtues to these four. Of special importance is that the Stoics conceived virtue as a kind of knowledge, so that courage, for example, was the knowledge of what should be properly endured. This is not to say that courage does not also involve action, such as fighting in battle, but only that the virtue of courage is primarily constituted by knowledge.

Yet despite acknowledging that the virtues are multiple, the Stoa also seemed to embrace the idea that what are called virtues, plural, are really aspects or manifestations of a single virtue. Whoever possesses one virtue possesses them all. Why might the Stoics commit themselves to this view of the unity

The four cardinal virtues: wisdom, temperance, courage, and justice.

of the virtues? Their position makes more sense if we can appreciate that the nature of virtue is a kind of knowledge, and knowledge resides in the mind. And the mind, just like the virtues, is a unity.

THE UNITY OF THE MIND

For the Stoics, virtue is a fixed character in the soul. The steadfastness of the soul is what accounts for this consistency of virtue. The Stoics were insistent that the soul possesses a fundamental unity. This belief was reflected in how the mind works. So, when you see someone who is conflicted about something, this is not to be explained by an appeal to two different and antagonistic desires within them. For example, on a conventional understanding, a man who wants to eat food that is bad for him, say a whole chocolate cake, will have the desire to both eat the cake and not eat the cake, and this tug of war wages a battle for supremacy. Whichever desire wins determines the action taken—eating or not eating. But the Stoic conception of this struggle is not of two simultaneous, competing actions, but rather of a singular alternating and unstable mind.

The man considers eating the cake, then not eating it, until at some point the issue is either settled, by devouring the cake, or perhaps he draws out his temptation to another date, when he will again be subjected to the tensions of his unstable mind.

Several related results come from viewing the mind as a unity in this way. One is that the way the mind should be cultivated is singular as well, since to choose what is good and virtuous is nothing other than having a rightly ordered mind—which is the same way of saying that one has a mind possessing virtue. Now, this is far from establishing that the only thing we should value is virtue, but it does show that, for the Stoic, the attainment of virtue was a very significant achievement, conferring a power to act correctly and wisely in all situations.

VIRTUE AND HAPPINESS

The attainment of virtue is identified with the achievement of happiness. Like other Greek schools of philosophy before and after them, the Stoics believed that the aim of human life is happiness. The disagreement among the various schools was over how this was to be attained. In Stoicism, it is obtained through virtue, understood as the acquisition and practice of thoughts and activities that lead to excellences of the mind and character. Once these have been achieved, happiness is achieved.

THE SAGE AND THE IMPROVER

Though in theory the attainment of virtue is the priority of the Stoic life, this does not mean that in practice this will be easy or even an achievable expectation. The rare practitioner who gained the wisdom which virtue involves was called a sage. It is unclear from the Stoic texts that we have whether real sages were ever found walking the earth or whether they were merely posited as exemplars, an aspirational ideal. At any rate, what is certain is that at the very least they are extremely rare. Stoicism is not for everyone. It makes no claims to be easy.

But despite this strict expectation to conform to the ideal of the sage, Stoicism still left room for the imperfect. The Stoics even coined a name for the student who continually strives for perfection, calling them an "improver." The word they used in Greek was *prokoptōn*, which literally means "cutting forward." Thus, the idea is that one advances, metaphorically, by cutting one's way forward. The direction and orientation are toward virtue, and there is progress, even if the destination is never reached.

The wise man is said to do well at everything. He is, the Stoics would say, a perfected human being and thus he acts out the part of a human being well, doing everything he does in accordance with virtue.

VICE

If virtue is what we ought to pursue, vice is what we ought to shun. The difference between vice and virtue is absolute: there is no third ethical category between them. In other words, if you are not virtuous, you are vicious. The "improver," as he advances toward the status of a sage, is still enveloped by vice. To understand this, imagine two drowning men. One is an arm's length from the surface and the other is hundreds of fathoms down. Both, the Stoic observes, are equally drowning. This analogy is meant to show that the vicious man who has made some moral progress, in being closer to the "surface" of virtue, is in the same state as the man deep in the ocean of vice. Vice and virtue are opposites of a type, because with the presence of one is the absence of the other. The vices reflect a disturbance and disorderliness in the soul, which is uncharacteristic of virtue—an ordering of the soul in accordance with nature and reason.

FREE WILL AND DETERMINISM

In Stoicism significant weight is given to Zeus and fate. On its own this presents no problems, but when combined with an ethical theory which promotes the continuous choosing of what is virtuous over what is not, determinism is a difficulty that needs to be reconciled. Determinism, in its simplest terms, is the belief that everything that occurs has been determined to occur by what has happened before it. In the case of ethical decisions, this would mean that we are not really choosing the good or bad, but whether the circumstances of our brain, or the conditions of the world, or other combinations of things, have determined the way we did or will act. The early Stoics attempted to reconcile this tension between the role of fate and our own agency by offering some memorable images.

Think, for example, of a dog tied to the back of a cart. An ancient cart was something quite formidable and heavy, itself pulled by one or more horses. When the cart begins to move the dog perceives the movement and begins to move along with it. There is an alternative, however, in which the dog resists the movement but is nevertheless compelled to trot along behind the wagon because it is unable to resist the bulk and momentum

Stoics believed individual free will is compatible with fate.

Free Will and Fate

One dog goes along voluntarily with the wagon.

One dog goes along involuntarily with the wagon.

Both dogs will go in the direction of the wagon.

---

of the vehicle. From a certain perspective, the actions of both dogs would seem to be the same. Yet with the dog which chose to go along with the wagon, it seems to have saved itself some trouble by voluntarily choosing to submit itself to the inevitable motion of the wagon. There is a clear sense of fate in this analogy, and the importance of psychologically preparing oneself for whatever fate one finds oneself in.

In another example, a cylinder is lying on the ground. It will not move of itself but will if given a push. Unlike other shapes, say a rock or a triangle, the cylinder has within its nature the propensity to roll. But it must be given that initial movement in order to start rolling. The force of the analogy amounts to this. The initial movement causing the cylinder to move comes from outside, and this corresponds to the external and prior causes that act upon us in a certain way. Those factors exist and exert true influence upon us. But once the cylinder is rolling, so to speak, our own nature, involving choice, takes over. That initial force is no longer operative; it has been taken into the cylinder for its own purposes.

These two analogies vividly capture the tension involved in the context between free will and determinism. The Stoics were clearly trying to maintain the truth of both free will and fate, and we can say, using a modern label, that they were "compatibilists." They affirmed that there was a harmony between the demands of fate and the choices of the human will.

Virtue is what we set our lives in pursuit of, even if we sometimes or usually fall short of its attainment. It is the North Star which we aim for. Having attained it, it cannot be taken away. This is one of the reasons which commended virtue to the Stoics, for, unlike riches, reputation, family, and other so-called external goods, it is identified with the very self and cannot be lost as long as one is living. Virtue alone can merit happiness for the human condition, and its opposite, vice, must be shunned and eliminated.

CHAPTER 4
Nature

"Nature" is a tricky term. In its common usage it usually refers to either the world around us which has not been fashioned by human intervention, or is the distinct character that each thing possesses, such as the nature of a human or the nature of a tree. For the Stoics, the first definition, of nature as the sum total of things that exist, was the conception they were concerned with.

The Stoics developed an interesting ontology, a Greek word simply meaning the "study of things that are or exist." They began with the idea that everything that exists is something. After this, and using a simplified version of a classification system used by Aristotle, they placed every "something" into one of two categories: body or bodiless (with perhaps a third "neither" category, for fictional things like centaurs). Into the bodiless, things without any physicality, they placed the sayables (words), void, place, and time. Body has four categories: substrate, quality, state, and relation. All four categories belong to each body. A substrate is what we might call the thing itself, the main thing we have in mind when we are referring to something, such as a horse or flower. The quality of the horse might be large and white, or, for the flower, yellow. The state of the horse, for example, could be well-conditioned and trained. Its relation could be "owned by Socrates" or "offspring of Bellerophon." Whether they belonged to the body or bodiless (or neither) category, all things were therefore "something." This commonsensical feature was an acknowledgment that in order to exist a thing has to be something, of some kind, in the first place.

THE PLACE OF MANKIND IN NATURE

At first glance, it may appear that these distinctions, while they have a kind of utility and logic to them, do not seem to directly relate to what we know of Stoicism so far. But there is a very important relationship with the ethical that this categorization involves. This is the commitment that man must live in accordance with nature, a concept in Stoic thought that is mentioned as frequently as living in accordance with virtue. What do these two ideas have in common? The general idea is that, among all the things that exist (excepting the gods), humans alone are rational or even capable of rationality. Human nature, in other words, is oriented toward the rational, and to reject this rational inclination is also to reject nature. To live in accord with reason, at least for humans, is to live in accord with nature. Chapter 6 will explore this in more detail, but this doctrine of living in accordance with nature presupposes that humans and the world we live in has been designed. The high god, Zeus, is a principle which suffuses all the universe, keeping it together by the power of his being.

THE FOUR ELEMENTS

The Stoics, following Plato and Aristotle, among others, thought that all physical things were constituted by the four elements of fire, air, earth, and water. These elements are not equal, however, as the Stoics placed fire above the rest, positing that the other three are made when fire is altered in one way or another. Fire was the primary element in the sense that the other three elements were a modification of fire in the appropriate way. Nevertheless, these four elements, in combination or singly, make up everything that has a body of one kind or another. When it comes to dividing the four elements, fire and air are active while earth and water are passive.

AIR AND FIRE

These two elements play a strange and idiosyncratic role within the Stoic cosmos. Since physical things are made up of combinations of fire, air, water, and earth, and only fire and air are active elements, it makes sense that these two elements possess great importance. The Stoics described these two elements as the

BODY

sustaining forces in the world. They maintain the order of the world, not only for other things but for themselves. Air and fire are also described as the cold and the hot, and by blending them to different ratios, these elements, as breath, were supposed to result in different properties or effects. We are familiar with human and animal breath being both hot and composed of air, so there is reason to suppose that the Stoics based their belief on this observation.

Although fire and air work in tandem, fire is the most important of the elements. It has a vitality that imparts life to all living things. Although we are often used to thinking of fire as random and destructive, the Stoics made a distinction among two different types of fire. There is, on the one hand, what we think of as fire, the flaming element that consumes other objects, using them as fuel for itself. On the other hand, pointing to the sun and to the fire that resides within living bodies and gives them warmth, there is also a fire that is life-giving, constructive, and intelligent. This nobler fire is what is seen throughout the cosmos, bestowing vitality and order on everything.

Fire and air mixed together as breath permeate the entire universe. This breath, depending on how it interacts with the physical bodies it resides in, has a tension to it. One could consider it as a kind of invisible and immaterial glue, with the additional characteristic that, unlike normal glue, breath brings with it an orderliness of design and structure. What gave fire and air this tension? According to Chrysippus, fire is hot and air is cold. Just as modern physics would admit, heat expands and cold contracts. Since breath is a mixture of hot and cold, and these expand and contract respectively, many different varieties of expansion and contraction are possible. These different expansions and contractions are the movements of the ratio of breath that is unique to each kind of thing.

What this amounts to in the real world is the idea that fire and air sustain the earth and water in a certain configuration, resulting in a particular kind of thing. For instance, the sustaining of the earth and water in one configuration of fire and air could be manifested in a tree, while the sustaining of water alone might show itself as a river. This sustaining is again identified with a tension of the expanding of hot fire and the contraction of cold air, fitting and characteristic to a given object, living or inanimate.

THE SOUL'S COMPOSITION

The soul is breath, where this is understood to be a mixture of fire and air. The soul is a particularly lucid example of the Stoic commitment to explaining individual entities as different configurations of breath interacting with matter. The Stoics called the most important aspect of the soul the *hegemonikon*, or ruling part. The ruling part, as its name implies, gives order and is the central rationality of the soul. This ruling part is like an octopus, but with seven rather than eight tentacles stretching out from the human body. Sight, hearing, touch, smell, and taste account for five of the "tentacles." These are described as a particular kind of breath leading from the ruling part to the sense organ in question. For example, breath leading from the ruling part to the eyes is sight, or from the ruling part to the ears is hearing. Of the two remaining tentacles, one is reproduction, leading from the ruling part to the genitals, and the last is speech, moving from the ruling part to the vocal organs. What these traits have in common is that, like tentacles, they can move by becoming more tense or more relaxed. This movement accounts for the various impressions or activities uniquely suited for that faculty of the soul.

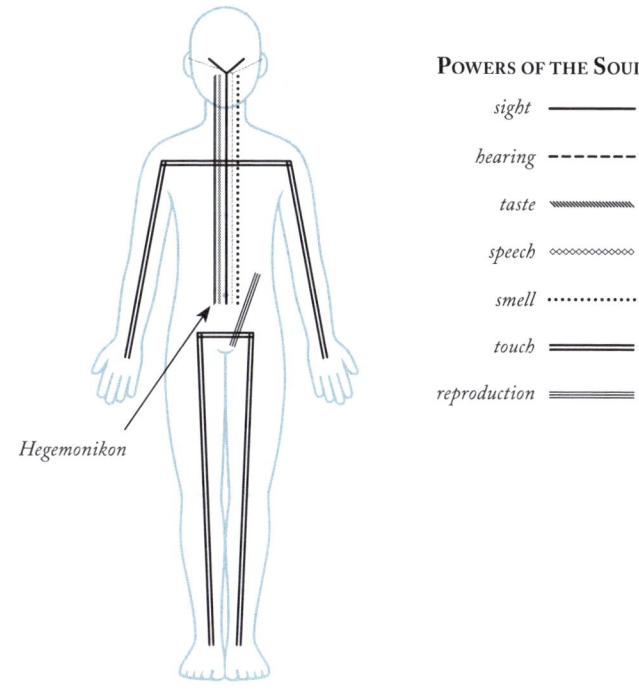

Hegemonikon

Powers of the Soul
- sight
- hearing
- taste
- speech
- smell
- touch
- reproduction

BLENDING AND MIXTURE

From the Stoic perspective, the concepts of blending and mixture held considerable importance. We have already seen one aspect of this, where the soul is thought of as a blend of both air and fire. Another facet of the importance of blending is the relationship that fire, as an element, has with the entire universe, which it somehow permeates and fills with its presence. Lastly, whether and to what degree things can mix with each other plays a key role in Stoic thought in determining what we consider something to be.

In defending this conception of blending, the Stoics took some seemingly strange positions. When Chrysippus said "a drop of wine penetrates the whole ocean," he meant that the blending of the wine with the ocean meant the drop would be equally extended through all of the water. There is clearly an analogous relationship between this bold claim and the more general role of breath in Stoicism as a force that permeates everything. The blending of the wine with the sea is supposed to show that when something is of the right substance, it can imperceptibly become inseparable from what it is blended with, just as in the case of breath in the cosmos.

ETERNAL RECURRENCE

Given the primacy of the element of fire, it might come as no surprise to learn that fire in Stoic thinking plays a role in the end of the universe. It does not do this in a chaotic, uncontrolled way, however. On the contrary, the end of the world for Stoics would come as a result of the rational principle of fire permeating the cosmos completely. When it has pervaded every last corner of the universe, this celestial fire will have consumed everything there is in flames.

This is not the final end of the universe, though. The cosmos will come again, created anew by the fire once more. The universe goes through this cycle of destruction and creation continuously, always being generated on the same rational principles. Interestingly, the Stoics held that each regeneration was always the same. A horse or a person existing now will be the same horse or person in the infinity of universes to come. Chrysippus clarified that everything that is will not be replicated in exactly the same way, but that any differences will be minor. A man in this iteration of his existence with moles on his face may not have them in his next life, he said, but he would still be the same man.

Because of their belief that fire was the supreme ordering principle, it makes sense that the Stoics argued that the end of everything would be the result of a cosmic conflagration. It was equally plausible, they thought, that the universe would not just be reborn again and again, but that it would be the same rational universe each time, destroyed and then created by the "noble fire" that gives order and vitality to all things.

Another consideration for the Stoics was their commitment to fate. Remember that we saw in Stoicism a dual allegiance to free will and fate (see Chapter 3). Stoics believed that, right before the final conflagration of all matter, the cosmos will be in the same configuration as at all previous and subsequent apocalypses. This follows from the commitment to fate—when things are arranged physically in one way, a certain and fixed result will necessarily follow from that prearrangement.

The acknowledgment of the idea of eternal recurrence had a therapeutic benefit for Stoics as well. The present gains a distinct importance, because it is only the present in which we live. This is true regardless of which recurrence we are living in and affects us the same no matter how long we live. The cyclical nature of the universe ensures that we will come back to the same moments and experiences over and over again.

CHAPTER 5
The Passions

The emotions, or passions, are an inescapable and pervasive feature of human activity. A rich life, it is often assumed, will have its share of good and bad emotions. While the Stoics certainly would admit that the emotions are well established in human life, they would vehemently disagree that human life is better with them or concede that our lives are impossible without them. For the Stoic, humans are best served by the elimination of the emotions.

The Stoic attack on the passions should not be understood as emotional repression, an unhealthy practice which ultimately does us some kind of harm. The Stoic resistance to emotions goes much deeper. It is an attempt at the total extirpation, or rooting up, of the passions. To go to the root of the passions, we must first discover what they are.

THE NATURE OF THE PASSIONS

The etymology of the word "passion" comes from the Latin *pati*, meaning "to suffer." This is something the Stoics incorporated into their conception of the passions. The passions are something we endure, at the hands, so to speak, of something else. This implies we are not in control of our passions—they happen to us and we receive them passively, and they are not something we actively choose, pursue and engage in. Think of how anger or joy are not something you choose, but you find yourself in one of these states. This identifies something from the get-go which will be unacceptable to a Stoic. The source of a good and happy life is nothing but virtue, as we have seen in Chapter 3. If one accepts this, it raises two problems with emotions, one with their origin and the other in their effect. The origin of an emotion is something outside the virtuous fortress of the self. Virtue lies in the self and the cultivation of character through a life lived in accordance with reason. An emotion, whatever else it is, is something quite distinct from a virtue. The more problematic element in the emotions, though, is that they disturb the cultivation of virtue in the soul.

THE DIVISION OF THE PASSIONS

Although the emotions were numbered in different ways by the Stoics, the primary division is into four categories, into which all others fit. They are desire, fear, pain, and pleasure. The reason for this four-fold categorization is that the Stoics believed all emotions are essentially illusory. In other words, they are based on a false appearance. Appearances are generally present now or are future-facing, and appear as good or bad. We naturally feel compelled to pursue what we perceive as good and to shun or avoid what we perceive as bad. In the case of the emotions, this means that desire and pleasure are perceived as good, and fear and pain are perceived as bad. Good and bad are not the only axis upon which the emotions are scaled. There is also a temporal structure to them. Fear and desire are both oriented toward the future, while pain and pleasure concern the present. When we combine all the descriptions, we have a neat schematic of emotions. Present bad things are pains, present goods are pleasures, future goods are desires, and future bad things are fears.

The Passions, or Emotions

	Good	**Bad**
Present	Pleasure	Pain
Future	Desire	Fear

VIRTUE AND PASSIONS

The passions can be approached from different angles, but the most important consideration of them is in comparison to virtue. Nothing in life is as important to the Stoic as the pursuit and attainment of virtue. But the passions raise a challenge to the unique position of virtue. Most significantly, they tell us something else is to be pursued, namely what is viewed as a present good (pleasure), or a future good (desire). In doing this we supplant virtue from its unique and exclusive role as the aim of rational human life. But, for the Stoic, virtue will have no competitors, no other "gods" to whom we will give worship. It must be the sole and shining beacon to which we fix our course, and if we are distracted by something else, we are led off course to viciousness and irrationality.

The four passions.

PASSIONS AS A TYRANT

The passions were conceived of as disturbances of the soul. They were in this way opposed to reason because they hindered the natural use of the soul. But it is not merely that the emotions throw a wrench into the gears of the properly ordered soul. That would be enough on its own to shun the emotions, but this is not their most pernicious aspect. The most destructive part of the passions is that they lead us away and astray. Many of us are familiar enough with having our anger get the better of us, or of being led into some quite foolish activity for the sake of a love interest. In episodes like this, we say things such as, "I wasn't myself," "I couldn't help it," or "anger made me do it." The Stoics would agree with this assessment, and point to it as evidence of the way that the emotions work against us.

THE PHYSICAL NATURE OF EMOTIONS

Recall that the Stoics were materialists. Everything that exists is of a material nature in some way. This is also the case with psychological states, which can be described mentally or physically. Pain and fear are contractions of the ruling part, while pleasure and desire are swellings. The contraction is a physical shrinking away from what is not wanted in the case of pain and fear, while swelling is a physical growth toward the objects of what is seen as good for pleasure or desire.

The Material Nature of the Passions

	Present	Future
Contraction	Pain	Fear
Swelling	Pleasure	Desire

Chrysippus was of the opinion that the ruling part of the soul was situated in the heart, not the brain. The evidence he brought forth for this view is that when we experience an emotion such as fear, anger, or excitement, these all seem to occur directly in the chest.

APPEARANCES AND PASSION

A passion is something that is fundamentally irrational. One way to understand this is to see how they work entirely by appearances. An appearance may or may not be true, but the emotion is beholden to following it—this is simply what an emotion is. If, on the other hand, something is accepted or pursued because it is rational, then there simply is no need for the passion; reason is enough. In his work *On Anger*, Seneca counsels an imaginary interlocutor about taking vengeance for the murder of a mother. Vengeance is an emotion with anger and a desire to act out that anger. Seneca instead offers the alternative of justice. Justice, as a virtue, is something that is pursued in accordance with reason, while vengeance is pursued by an irrational and perhaps insatiable need for personal emotional satisfaction. Seneca points out that the duty we owe to our mothers upon their murder is not something that can be discharged through vengeance. Instead, it is found in justice, and with the greater benefit that it is rational and virtuous.

REASON IS SUFFICIENT

The virtuous person, we know, follows reason in all his deliberations and actions. Virtue and reason are what we look to in determining what is to be done, in other words. This exclusive role is reserved for virtue and reason only. But the passions are something else. And the passions are pernicious in that they sneak in and attempt to deceive us with an appearance. Now, if the appearance happens to be in accord with what reason already tells us is actually going on, then this makes our acknowledgment of the appearance of the emotion unnecessary. We have reason to tell us, rendering passion a superfluous element.

THE ELIMINATION OF THE PASSIONS

If the passions are to be avoided because they obstruct the true good of virtue and its attainments, how do we do this? Remember that the Stoics consider the mind to be a simple unity. This means that on the physical level, emotions are not some additional aspect of the mind, but are corruptions or distortions of the unified mind. A deviation from the mind rather than something substantial in themselves. But on the psychological level, this manifests in faulty thoughts. So, while a passion is a physical distortion of the ruling part of the soul, it is at the same time a mental disturbance. In order to address the problem of emotions, the Stoics did not have at their disposal means to fix the physical side of the equation. Instead, they focused on the mental aspect.

Since the mind is a unity, and it is essentially rational, this requires that in the case of the passions something irrational and untoward is happening in the mind to upset its proper order. In this way of thinking, the cure for passions is to understand that the underlying cause of any given emotion is untrue. This is an indication of what can be called the intellectualist approach to therapy. In other words, whatever is wrong with the mind must principally be dealt with as it concerns the thoughts we have.

An emotion is nothing other than a disordered and unwelcome thought, one that has to somehow be "unthought." For instance, if there is anxiety and fear over some project that has to be turned in for school or work on a quick deadline, under the Stoic scheme this would be described as a "future bad thing" from the perspective of the one with the fear. The proper perspective, however, would be to measure the importance of this fear with what really matters. And what really matters for a Stoic? Virtue. So, we measure our fear as it stands in relation to virtue. When we consider this, we come to realize, or should come to realize, that the fear holds no value in relation to virtue. Virtue is our ultimate and only value. To fall under the sway of an emotion is to value the object of that emotion more than virtue. Thus we become angry, thinking that the vengeance we will exact on our enemy is of value, though only virtue is valuable. We become sad, thinking that we have become deprived of a favorite possession through theft or breakage.

In all such cases, what is happening is that we mistakenly attribute value to something equal to that which virtue alone possesses. We treat a pleasure, pain, fear, or desire as something which can in some way be as valuable as virtue. This is, of course, a mistake, and the way to eliminate this error in judgment is to focus back on the nature of virtue itself and compare this accurate perspective on virtue with our inaccurate assessment of emotions.

This mode of philosophical therapy focuses on changing the fundamental way we think, and to change the way we think must begin with assigning the proper value to things. If we do not acknowledge virtue as the supreme value, or, alternatively, we grant the object of our anger or lust a value, any value at all, we err greatly. The Stoics would readily grant that saying this is much easier than following it through, but remember that they are the ones who say that to achieve the status of a sage is a feat worthy of many generations. The proper elevation of the pursuit of virtue and the corresponding debasement of all passion is not something that will come easily. When we get cut off by an oblivious driver we are certainly tempted to value telling him off or making an obscene gesture toward him. This is because we value vengeance over virtue, not only in this particular episode, but generally. Fundamentally, somewhere deep in our internal convictions, we believe that there is value in pursuing and acting out the anger we have in such a situation. This situation is only a token of what we believe about the world. We can only remove the false view of the emotions when we eliminate them entirely.

EUPATHEIAI

In addition to the emotions, the Stoics also made a place for the so-called "good emotions," which they termed *eupatheiai*. These are available only to the Stoic sage and differ chiefly in that they are necessarily connected with virtue and wisdom. Unlike the emotions discussed already, these good emotions are not essentially connected to false beliefs about what is good and valuable.

"Good Emotions," or *Eupatheiai*

	Good	Bad
Present	Joy	[none]
Future	Wish	Caution

CHAPTER 6
The Gods

The divine is an intriguing topic in Stoicism as it combines the physics of the cosmos and contributes to our understanding of the role of rationality both in ourselves and the world around us. The Stoics adapted the role of the traditional Greek god, Zeus, and in his position of providence he inhabited the world he created.

THE DESIGN OF THE UNIVERSE

To begin with, the universe is essentially rational. This means not only that there is design—and therefore purpose—to everything that exists, it also signifies that humans are rational in their nature as well. The explanation for this is that Zeus, intelligence, or fate, for they are all an interchangeable concept, has designed the universe. He is in some way either identified with or becomes fire, or breath, and through this special element creates and sustains the world. The four elements, from the lightest to the heaviest, are created by Zeus in succession: fire, air, water, and then earth. The successive nature of these elements arises from the fact that they are transformed by Zeus from one into another, air from fire, water from air, and earth from water.

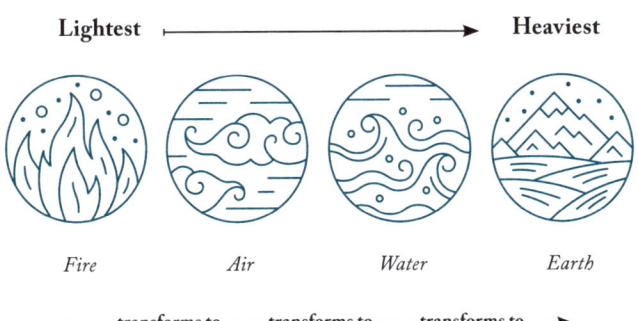

FOUR ELEMENTS

Lightest → Heaviest

Fire — Air — Water — Earth

⊢ transforms to — transforms to — transforms to →

There is a providential wisdom to the preservation of this matter, which undergoes successive transformations, when, for example, living things come to be and die. The four elements are only part of the creation story, however, as it is Zeus as breath which manifests in different ways in different substances. He binds different things in different ways, as the breath can take on different characteristics depending on what kind of joining needs to be done. Some of the primary distinguishing categories are man, animal, plant, and inanimate matter, which will each receive a different type of breath to give them their characteristic nature.

The world will end in a great fire, and from the theological point of view, as opposed to the physical perspective (though these should not be taken to conflict), what happens is that Zeus, as the "soul" of the universe, continues to suffuse and permeate the cosmos. He does this to greater or lesser degrees, depending on what physical matter he happens to manifest in. At some point in the future this process will be fulfilled, and Zeus will have completely used up the physical matter of the universe, like fuel in a fire. This is the point where the entire

CYCLICAL VIEW OF THE UNIVERSE

cosmos ends in a fiery apocalypse, since the purpose of Zeus has been accomplished. From this the world will begin anew.

THE DIVINE AND THE PHYSICAL

A strict separation between Zeus and the matter he inhabits, chiefly in the form of divine fire, appears to be an impossibility. This is to say that Zeus is material or completely dependent on the matter in the universe. When he is fire, or breath (air and fire together), this should not be taken as the typical fire or breath we experience. Rather, Zeus, as this fire, is fundamentally rational and imparts this rationality to whatever he comes into contact with. This captures the physical and spiritual dualism so frequently seen in Stoicism—an acknowledgment that at one and the same time there are material and psychological forces operating as one, though manifesting differently depending on the aspect under which they are considered. Zeus confers rationality as the psychological principle, but as fire he gives warmth and motion to all things.

Zeus's interaction with the universe shows us a few things. One is that the providence of Zeus is absolute; one might even say it increases with time as his power comes to superintend more and more of the universe. The sustainment of the universe depends on the god being everywhere in some way, for otherwise some part of the universe would not be able to function, much less exist.

Since the universe goes through a succession of ultimate fires in which everything is burned away and then Zeus regenerates everything again, this suggests that everything is impermanent except Zeus and these world cycles.

In Chapter 4 we talked about the doctrine of eternal recurrence, where, after the destruction of the universe through fire, an almost identical new one is created by Zeus. This indicates that Zeus's rational plan for the universe is consistent. He does not arbitrarily decide a different and random plan for the universe every time. This may suggest something else quite interesting about the nature of Zeus and his providence: that even he may not be able to escape the inevitability of the fate that he is part of. The reason is that the nature of Zeus, before the world is created on each occasion, is always going to be the same. Since the Stoics are determinists, they would say that prior conditions necessarily determine what follows. In this case, what is prior is the nature of Zeus. From this, it would seem that necessarily the same world would always be brought into creation. The prior condition of Zeus's immutable nature requires that what follows always follows and in the same way.

THE STOICS AND BELIEF IN THE GODS

The Stoics believed in the gods. The question remains as to what reasons motivated this belief in the divine. In Cicero's work *On the Nature of the Gods*, different representatives from the Greek schools take turns arguing for their account of the divine. The Stoic representative is Balbus, and he gives several arguments for belief in the gods.

PROOF OF THE GODS

The prelude to these arguments is that belief in the gods is inborn. As proof of this claim, Cicero notes that all men, or at least the vast majority of them, believe in the gods. This implies that there is an instinct within us which naturally develops into belief in the existence of the gods. From this there is no need to develop a series of premises with a conclusion. It is almost like saying that since there is a great desire for the satisfaction of our thirst, there must be something like water which exists to satisfy that thirst. This argument also establishes a strong connection between two favorite themes of Stoicism: nature and reason. What is believed, the existence of the gods, is believed by the nature of inborn instinct, but this belief is perfectly rational.

BALBUS'S ARGUMENTS FOR THE EXISTENCE OF THE GODS

Before continuing, Balbus announces that he is following Cleanthes, second leader of the Stoa, in his further arguments as to how a conception of the gods comes into men's minds. The first of these arguments concerns the apprehension of future events: That the future can be known and communicated to humans is an indication of supernatural foreknowledge.

The second argument relates to what can be termed the "Goldilocks universe" and holds that the conditions and habitat of the universe and Earth, such as the fertility of our planet's soil and its liveable climate, are not accidental. They could only have been made so for the benefit of mankind by gods who not only existed but knew and cared about mortal needs.

OLYMPIAN GODS

Zeus   *Hera*   *Ares*

Aphrodite   *Dionysus*   *Hermes*

Balbus's third argument appeals to the terrifying displays of power seen in nature. These include lightning and storms, and presumably such events as earthquakes, volcanic eruptions, and catastrophic floods. Since this follows the "Goldilocks universe" argument in Cicero's book, it can be seen as its complementary counterpart. As the Goldilocks argument appealed to the good things we see on Earth, inexplicable by human agency, so too the bad things we see, also beyond human power and comprehension, seem to require a divine and omnipotent power behind their operation.

THE GODS 69

Artemis

Poseidon

Athena

Demeter

Hephaestus

Apollo

The fourth and last argument for the existence of the gods is the design seen in the natural world. This is manifest in the seasons on Earth and the paths of the heavenly bodies. In the case of the universe, Balbus provides the analogy of a house in which we see how the furniture is organized and, from that, can reasonably infer that someone made and arranged those items in place.

While all of these examples can be called arguments for the existence of the gods, more properly they should be understood as ways that the concept of the gods is placed in our minds.

The idea is that, in the normal course of human life, we come across phenomena for which there is no obvious explanation and which, in due course, lead to a belief in the gods. These can be formulated as arguments or evidence for the gods, but it is more accurate to look at them as experiential inclinations. By living a normal human life, reason will naturally expose us to these ways of coming to a concept of the gods.

ZENO'S TREE OF FLUTES

As we have seen, the Stoics believed that the universe is filled with the divine substance of Zeus. This divine substance, conceived of as fire or breath, is also a manifestation of the rational principle of the universe. It gives shape and purpose to everything, but it is also the cause of rationality in humans. To defend the rationality of the world, in other words, is to defend the existence and rationality of Zeus.

To explain this, Zeno offered an analogy. Imagine an olive tree, he said, where some of its branches were also flutes, and that these flutes played music. Although it was only the flute parts of the tree that played music, we would have no hesitation, he argued, in attributing to the entire tree an understanding of music. In the same way, since man is part of the universe, and the universe is what gives birth to man, it must be the case that the universe itself is intelligent.

PROVIDENTIAL INTERCONNECTEDNESS

The Stoics were quite keen on the idea that all things in the world are connected and have a relationship. This will be explored properly in Chapter 7, when we will discuss the kinship Stoics saw among men, but also the world more generally. The Stoics had a view of the gods' interaction with the cosmos that could be described as providential rather than interventional. That is, the world evidences a design that cares for all things, and more particularly, looks out for the benefit of mankind. This design is baked in from the beginning—the gods do not intervene with miracles to fix or provide for the earth. So it was that Chrysippus believed that even things we think are purposeless or annoying possess a benefit for the universe. Bedbugs, he thought, are provided to keep us from sleeping too much. Vermin are nature's way of helping us to maintain cleanliness. It was not only practical functions which the world evidences. Beauty and variety for their own sake are features pervasive throughout all of nature. The peacock, Chrysippus insisted, is the best example of nature's propensity for beauty. On this understanding, the tail explains the entire reason this kind of creature was created. In other words, the bird was created to fit the beautiful tail, not the other way around.

This type of reason is the exact opposite of how we would tend to think of the peacock today, but it goes to show the pervasive providence of the gods which Stoics saw in the world.

CHAPTER 7
Politics

The Stoic theory of the universe and nature within it has a degree of reasonable appeal. After all, who does not want to live in accordance with whatever we have been born for, in line with what is rational, and pursue virtue as the highest form of life? But this commitment to what is natural to man also involves some very unconventional thinking.

ZENO'S RADICAL SOCIETY

In Zeno's book *Republic*, of which only scattered passages remain, he described the ideal political community. In this work he advocated that all men treat each other as neighbors and fellow citizens. What unites all people in a city, he argued, is they share a common human nature. However, this unity is not without conditions. Wicked people are estranged from each other and from those who are virtuous. It is only the virtuous who are capable of sharing the city as friends and brothers. The fellowship of this city is so radical, in fact, that incest is not even forbidden since this practice can be observed with wild animals. Zeno's work was the target of much criticism in antiquity, but it gives us an insight into the scope of the Stoic project for humans, folding the political and ethical into a unified society.

Further important policies in the ideal Stoic state should also be mentioned, one affecting religious life and the others social life. The first is the abolition of temples. Of course, this may be construed as an act of impiety, but more likely it followed from the belief that no higher act of religious worship can occur than when man acts in accordance with reason. This can occur outside of temples, and, at any rate, a rational man can be rational anywhere at all.

The other notable features are the elimination of education and currency and the setting up of communal marriage. Now we must be careful as to what conclusions we draw from very limited fragmentary evidence, and in particular we only have a few sentences here and there about temples, currency, and education, so we are forced to fill in gaps in the record in a reasonable way. What seems to have been the motivation for the abolition of education and currency was a kind of faith in the natural inclinations of humans as rational creatures, outside of the constraints of formal training, and a desire to draw people away from money as the operative aim in community life. In the case of common marriages with multiple wives, the aim no doubt parallels the infamous reasoning seen in

Plato's *Republic*. In that work, having all things in common, including wives, was supposed to increase the closeness and brotherhood of the city.

APPROPRIATION: THE NATURAL DRAW TOWARD SELF-PRESERVATION

Nature is one of the enduring themes in Stoicism and it also plays an explicit role in the development of life in the universe. Chrysippus said that what an animal strives for, after having been brought into life, is to preserve its own physical constitution and the awareness it has of this constitution. This preservation begins with an "impulse," or instinct to live. At this initial stage, what is being described is that nature "appropriates" the individual creature, so that the proper impulse of self-preservation takes root. So what, then, is appropriation? A term derived ultimately from the Greek word for "house," it means to make something one's own, and in this respect the instinct to live leads, metaphorically speaking, to taking on more things as part of one's household. At this initial stage, what happens is that the individual has the impulse to self-awareness and self-preservation. This impulse is the primordial psychological movement in animals, as distinguished from plants. Before making other things part of the self, the self comes to be known to itself and begins to come into the full possession of itself.

This initial experience of nature for a creature is an awareness of its own body and a need for its preservation, but its natural orientation does not stop there. It also seeks to use its body and bodily parts for the design for which they have been set. A later Stoic would describe this in terms of becoming aware of what our bodies and parts are and what they are for. In his work collected as *Letters from a Stoic*, the Roman Stoic Seneca set out in Letter 121 two particularly memorable examples. The first is a baby which repeatedly falls when trying to stand up. The baby experiences pain and frustration in trying to walk, but it nevertheless is unflagging in its struggles. This is because the nature of human limbs is for them to walk. It is not comfort that a baby seeks, but the proper disposition of its life, in this case a body made for walking.

The second example is the upended turtle we encountered on page 32. The turtle wiggles on its back until it has righted itself. Both the baby and the turtle have an internal and invisible bent toward reason, understood as the fulfillment of their natures.

There is an undeniable kinship which we have with other humans. Along with Aristotle, the Stoics readily admitted that man is a social animal and that living in communities is an indispensable part of life. The foundation of these relationships can be seen in the family, where reproduction and care for one's offspring give us our first experience of the relations we have with our fellow humans. But the first and primary experience we have of nature and our relationship to it is the awareness we have of ourselves. This self-consciousness is the basis for all our further human relationships, and it is, as we will see, the center of our philosophical lives.

THE CIRCLES OF AFFECTION

We know that the Stoics believed that, as humans, we share a common bond. Logically, then, humans live in a community with all other humans, regardless of where we happen to have been born or who our blood relations happen to be. But there is still a problem. How can we have any ties or even obligations to people outside of our immediate association?

With this in mind, Hierocles, who was active around AD 430, gave vivid expression to the Stoic doctrine of appropriation. The first step, he said, is to recognize that the mind of each individual human is like the centerpoint of a circle, drawn around the self and the body. It is from the position of this first and smallest circle that we recognize and look out for our personal wellbeing. The circle of care we draw around our mind is so small that it is almost indistinguishable from the mind itself—in fact, we often make no distinction between our mind, our body, and ourselves.

A second circle, of considerable largeness compared to the first, is what we would call the immediate family: parents, siblings, spouse, and children. A third circle expands out and incorporates the extended blood relations of uncles, aunts, cousins, grandparents, and so forth. A fourth circle includes all other extended family members, a fifth local residents, a sixth fellow tribesmen, a seventh fellow citizens, an eighth neighboring tribespeople, and a ninth fellow countrymen. In the last and tenth circle are all human beings.

The most important takeaway from this elaboration of different circles is not the number or even the kind of humans in each layer, but Hierocles's admonition that we draw that

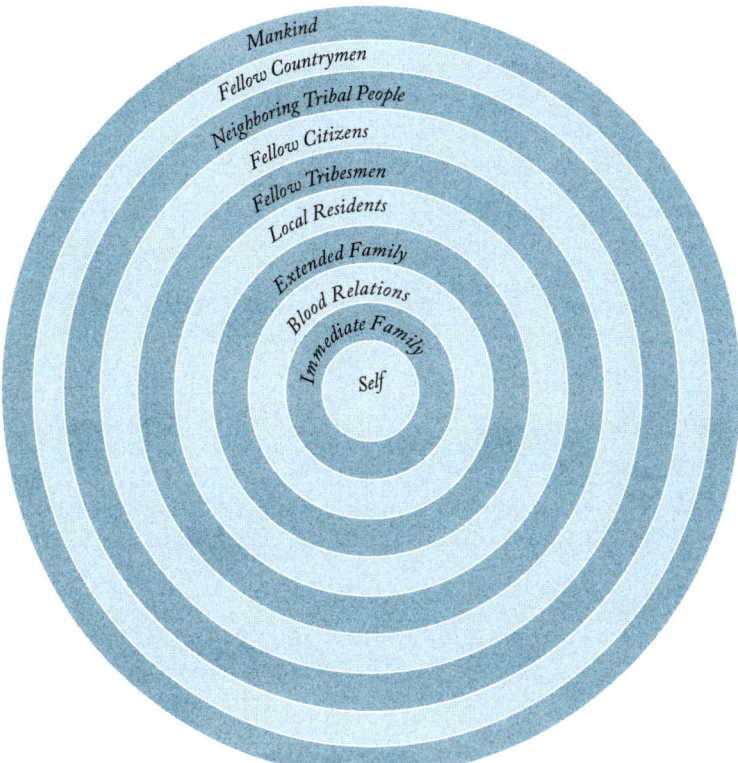

APPROPRIATION: CIRCLES OF HIEROCLES

farthest circle of humanity in toward us. In the process, all groups become closer than they would be without our attempt to draw them in. The layout of these concentric circles tells us that mankind loves to make associations at different levels of society, with lesser considerations for those who are farther out. Without necessarily making a judgment about the relative worth of the people in these different circles, the idea of appropriation asks that we bring people in closer to us. To treat people in the fourth layer as if they are in the third, and the third in the second, is the aim, not to treat everyone equally as yourself.

The overall picture is clear: those who are closer to us we treat better, those farther away we treat worse. There is more than just a suggestion that all people are importantly alike, sharing in human nature, which is itself a reflection of divine rationality. Each circle of Hierocles's scheme becomes progressively larger, with more people in an outer circle relative to an inside circle. The individual has a relation to all human beings and all human beings have a relation to the individual. This relationship is grounded in the natural reason found in all people.

With this discussion of the community of all mankind, it may come as a surprise that the Stoics were quite adamant in limiting this enfranchisement to humans alone. Animals, lacking the rational nature of mankind, are beings set out to serve the needs of mankind. Chrysippus, for example, argues that pigs have been created as a food source for mankind. The Stoic speaker, Cato, in Cicero's work *On Ends*, notes that some animals are obviously fashioned for the use of other animals, such as bees, which produce honey and pollinate plants for the benefit of other creatures. Most relevantly, animals lack the divine rationality which people partake of, so they have no share in the commonwealth of gods and men.

GODS AND MEN

The Stoics' conception of society reflects some very important beliefs about political life. They divided our societies, and our obligations to those societies, into two communities. The first is the community of gods and men, which has no boundaries; it is the entirety of the universe. Gods and men are both part of the same community, since both partake of the common nature of reason. Just as in any community where there are rulers and mere citizens, the gods are the rulers of all human beings. But there is also the particular earthly location in which we find ourselves. It is in this second community that we find ourselves living within the constraints of local traditions and with particular people.

In the context of people living under the beneficent rule of the gods, Stoics would claim that only the wise man is free, and everyone else is akin to a slave. The reason for this dire perspective is that it is only the wise who submit to reason, thereby submitting to the gods, who avoid the slavery of vice and ignorance.

NATURAL LAW

Under the community of gods and men, there is a common principle of rationality shared by both. The divine element is diffused throughout the universe, granting reason to nature itself. Among humans, this rational element shows itself in every society as something eternal and unchanging and available to everyone. It is a kind of "natural law" on how to act, and it is above and beyond any earthly political legislation. No city or state can supersede what this natural law dictates, as the natural law is supreme over all. As Cicero notes in his *Republic*, there will not be one law at Athens and another in Rome, but there will be one law for all peoples. This natural law transcends all times and places, an acknowledgment that there is one god and ruler over all.

Natural law has a way of manifesting itself in the minds of mankind, and law is a necessary element of society. This is because law prescribes what ought to be done by human beings who are politically organized by nature. Although law comes about in a sense from humans, who propose, enact, and interpret it, it is really from the reason dwelling within them that it is derived. For the Stoic, the divine is the cause and sustainer of the world, and we have a great responsibility to acknowledge and respond to the divine within the world and within ourselves. The world has been ordered by the gods and our role within that world is to help to further this order by appealing to our divine nature, reason.

CHAPTER 8

Seneca

Seneca was born in AD 1 in Córdoba, Spain. Along with his two brothers, he received the highest and most costly schooling of the day in Rome, an education usually reserved for the sons of the privileged elite hoping to take up legal and political careers. In addition to the expected training in public speaking, Seneca was also instructed in literature, history, poetry and, of course, philosophy.

Seneca's family background was impressive. The father, Seneca the Elder, was a public speaker, educated to a degree at least equal to his sons. Seneca's older brother, born Annaeus Novatus, but later known as Junius Gallio, was a proconsul of Achaia, Greece, in which capacity he met the Apostle Paul, as related in Acts 18:12. His younger brother was the father of the famous Roman poet Lucan, chronicler of the civil war between Julius Caesar and Pompey the Great.

CHAPTER 8

Seneca.

Sometime around early adulthood Seneca met the Greek Stoic philosopher Attalos, the most important of his teachers. Seneca studied Stoicism and became proficient in Greek under Attalos. He was also influenced at this time by the teachings of Quintus Sextius, a thinker whose work combined Stoicism with Pythagoreanism, which espoused a kind of mathematical mysticism. In this respect, Seneca was never a "pure" Stoic. But while his work and ideas borrowed from several schools of thought, it was undoubtedly Stoicism that had the greatest impact on him and to all intents and purposes he is remembered as a Stoic thinker.

Seneca was plagued by health issues throughout his life, by breathing problems in particular, an ironic malady given the importance of "breath" for Stoics as the intelligent force in the universe. But it was probably this same respiratory illness which saved his life. He became a prominent public figure in Rome, serving in the Senate, where his unbending commitment to traditional Roman—and Stoic—values of virtue and honor did not endear him to the less-than-Stoical Caligula, who became emperor in AD 37. It is said that Caligula considered having the sternly disapproving Seneca put to death, but was talked out of it by a member of the imperial court, who told him that Seneca was ill and going to die soon anyway. Following the emperor's assassination in AD 41, Seneca was forced into exile by Caligula's successor, Claudius, and remained away from Rome for the best part of a decade. When he was recalled, it was for the dubious honor of becoming tutor to Claudius's adopted teenage son, Nero.

Seneca remained Nero's advisor after he became emperor in AD 54, aged just 16, an association that was to prove disastrous and deadly. Despite a promising early start to his imperial reign, probably moderated by Seneca's influence, the increasingly unstable Nero had his younger brother poisoned and his mother assassinated, both viewed as obstacles to the free rein of his power. In AD 63, a dispirited Seneca stepped down from his official role as the imperial advisor, having failed to instill in Nero the Stoic virtues he hoped would make him a wise leader, turning his attention to his philosophical and literary work instead.

Emperor Nero.

Two years later, Seneca was implicated in an unsuccessful plot to overthrow Nero led by the statesman Gaius Calpurnius Piso. It is unlikely that Seneca was involved in the so-called Pisonian Conspiracy, Nero using it as a pretext to dispose of his former mentor, who was duly ordered to take his own life.

The Roman writer Tacitus recorded the drama of Seneca's death, which he portrayed as a model example of Stoic fortitude. After calmly dictating some last words and thoughts to a scribe, Seneca opened the veins on his own wrists and waited to bleed to death. When this took too long, he made cuts to his legs and climbed into a warm bath to hasten the flow of blood. All the while, he cautioned his assembled friends and family not to abandon the Stoic teachings he urged them to live by.

ADVICE FROM SENECA

Seneca's output as a writer was broad. He penned a number of what are commonly termed moral essays, on specific topics of ethical interest, and also produced grotesque and bloody tragedies as a playwright, wrote a natural history, and famously authored the *Apocolocyntosis* ("Pumpkinification"), a satire on the reign of Claudius where, on his death, he does not turn into a god—as it was claimed that emperors did—but a pumpkin.

But Seneca is best known today for the hundreds of letters he wrote to his friend Lucilius, many of which outlined his interpretation of Stoicism, and which will be the main focus of our analysis of him. The letters are often brief, congenial, and sometimes informal. In them we can see the personality of

Seneca shine through, and, more importantly, his wisdom. The precepts and insights they contain are applicable at all times and for all people. They serve as practical and useful guides to living well.

THE USE OF TIME

Time is of immense value to us. Yet we are not always in control of the time we have, or rather give. We have to go to work, clean the house, or prepare our tax returns. This is time that is "taken" from us. Yet, as Seneca points out, we do not always wisely spend the time that we do control. In Seneca's first letter, he reminds us that we should always think of time and how we use it in relation to our death. Death is not before us but behind us. This is because as we age, the time we have lived accumulates behind us, and the storehouse of time that has passed only becomes larger. So when death finally comes, we have found that it has been growing to maturity for a long time.

In his short essay *On the Brevity of Life*, Seneca notes that many people have a completely wrong conception of time when it comes to living. Instead of making the most of the time they have right now, he says, they reason that they can wait until they are older, when, in modern terms, they are retired. Seneca says that we should not look forward to the rest from labor that such a retirement would offer as there is no guarantee we will make it that far. Then there is the additional problem that, even if we do make it to an advanced age, we will have already lived most of our lives. Why wait to live, when life is a finite resource, when there is not an unending supply of years for our lives?

It is not only that time can slip away through our negligence. Life itself is quite difficult to live well. Living well is synonymous with happiness and it takes an entire lifetime to learn to live. The idle or frivolous things we spend our time on, according to Seneca, take away from the opportunity of learning to become happy.

The present plays an outsized role in our awareness of life, as it is what remains in our control. Even when it comes to the future, our present obligation to ourselves requires that we consider it with just as much clarity as the time that has passed.

DEATH

In Letter 4, Seneca reminds us that time is necessarily linked to our conception of death, and that death is something which eventually comes for us all. He gives us two reasons to come to terms with the idea of death. The first is that any evil that has an end is not a great evil. Since death has an end, a cessation of the evil that it presents, then it is not a great evil. In the second reason, Seneca analyzes the future aspect of death. Since it is in the future, there is an inevitable sense in which death is coming for us. However, either one of two things occurs in this scenario. The first possibility is that it has not come, in which case we are still living (just as we are now), or it does come, and death is over and done with. In this latter situation, when death has been consummated, we no longer have to worry about it.

Old age, too, is of particular concern, not only to those who are old, but to those who anticipate being so. Seneca reminds Lucilius that although his body gives him trouble, his mind has never been better than in his old age. The worry that we gradually fade away in old age, that there is a diminution of our powers, is not something to be feared. It is like a ship casting off its ropes at the dock, he says, gently gliding off to the seas.

Furthermore, rather than ignore death, we should think about it directly, he advises. Quoting Epicurus, Seneca tells us to "Meditate on death," or in an alternative formulation, "Go to the heavens." The idea is that in considering the nature of death we come to appreciate the freedom that it gives us. Considering death allows us to "unlearn death."

THE HIGHEST GOOD

Our focus and emphasis needs to be on our lives, considered as a unity and whole. Only when we have this in mind can we act correctly. In Letter 71, Seneca invokes the image of a painter who has every brush, every color, and an uncountable number of high-quality canvases on which to work. But if he does not possess a conception of what exactly he wants to paint, then he cannot, or should not, begin. Likewise, an archer can only hit something, anything, after he has already picked a target. The choice of target, its distance from the shooter, the velocity which it will be shot with, and even the type of bow and arrow, will only be determined when the target is decided upon.

Seneca's advice is in some ways representative of the Stoic

way of life. We must strive toward virtue. Virtue is an enveloping good, if we pursue it rightly. It has a way of transforming bad things and bad events into what is honorable and good.

In order to elevate virtue to its lone position as the good which we must pursue to attain happiness, Seneca fields the objection that this means we will not care about the multitude of apparently significant events going on around us, such as political maneuverings or social upheaval. The general answer is that all things in this current world are perishing. It is a law which everything and every person obeys, to come into being, to reach maturity, to grow old, and perish. This transitory nature of the world should prompt us to recognize that we are not exempt from this law, and that our eventual dissolution follows this same law in accordance with the design of nature.

More advice on how to live in the light of the single goodness that is virtue is offered in Letter 67. Here, Seneca clarifies that, while we should not seek out difficult and even painful circumstances, if we do find ourselves in them we should acquit ourselves well by acting bravely or patiently, or in whatever way virtue expects of us.

In a beautiful explanation discussing the nature of the good in Letter 66, Seneca explains that the divine intelligence permeates all things, sees all things at once, takes into account thought and action, and is a spirit that acts in accordance with nature and takes no account of human opinion. It is to this divine intelligence that we turn to live a life of virtue and reason. Wisdom, the expression of virtue and reason, is achieved through experience and practice.

CHAPTER 9
Marcus Aurelius

Marcus Aurelius (AD 121–180) ruled the Roman Empire for almost 20 years. He became emperor just before his 40th birthday and died aged 58. He was without doubt the most politically powerful Stoic that ever lived. He was the last of the "five good emperors," beginning with Nerva in AD 96, who controlled the Roman Empire during its period of greatest success and prosperity. His reign was spent almost entirely on military campaign, waging wars to secure and expand his empire's borders, and it was during this time that he wrote what is the best-known work of Stoic thought, *Meditations*.

Related through marriage to the emperors Trajan and Hadrian, Marcus was born in Rome to a wealthy patrician family. His father, Marcus Annius Varus, died when Marcus was three and he was raised by his mother, Domitia Calvilla, and his maternal grandfather, Marcus Annius Verus.

His noble ancestry ensured that Marcus was destined for a life of high political or military office, and his upbringing reflected this. Aged just six, he was enrolled into the Equestrian order of Roman knights by the sitting emperor, Hadrian. His formal education began a year later, his first tutors being called Geminus and Euphorus, of whom we know almost nothing other than that they were Roman and Greek respectively. Around this time, Marcus also became a priest of the Salii. This exclusive and prestigious order dedicated to the god of war Mars was limited to 12 members and only admitted aristocratic youths from well-connected families. It played a prominent role in some of the public religious ceremonies held in Rome throughout the year. It was while serving with the Salii that what was taken to be a prodigious omen occurred, when, during a ceremonial custom of throwing crowns on the couch of Mars, Marcus's own toss landed on top of the god's head.

As he approached his teenage years, Marcus's teacher Diognetus first introduced him to the edifying benefits of philosophy. His burgeoning interest in philosophy was nurtured by his next tutor, Marcus Cornelius Fronto, who would be his teacher and advisor for many years. It was while he was in his late teens that Marcus was adopted by Antoninus Pius, who he would succeed as Rome's emperor.

THE *MEDITATIONS*

He probably began to write the work he is best known for when he was in his late 40s and had been emperor for around a decade. Although the book's title is traditionally known as *Meditations*, Marcus called it *Ta eis heauton*, which translates as something like "to himself," which is an equally fitting name. It is a work of philosophical reflection, or meditation, in the sense that Marcus is looking to his past, present, and future with deep scrutiny. But it is better to think of the document as an examination of his conscience rather than as some kind of confession.

BOOK 1

The first part of *Meditations* is a book praising those who have contributed to Marcus's life to that point. Readers often skip this section, due to it being largely a list of personalized thanksgivings and it is seemingly irrelevant to a work of moral philosophy. But it is highly important in establishing that gratitude and awareness of where one has come from are necessary for an appropriate understanding of our own nature and where we are going.

BOOK 2

This book begins with a consideration of the trouble and aggravation we will encounter during the day. With typical Stoic fair-mindedness, it acknowledges that the annoying and even vicious people we have to deal with all share in the same divine intelligence, and that they cannot affect our own virtue.

A theme in this book is that we should recognize our own paltry existence—that we are here for only a short time, and that we do not make use of the time we have. The awareness of our own imminent death should determine everything we say and do.

BOOK 3

Marcus begins this book by acknowledging the nature of the human condition. We take it for granted that if we live long we will be in full control of our faculties. But we do not know when or if we will lose our minds through senility or lose control over our bodies. This fact should encourage us to be urgent in our activities, for disabling maladies can come well before death.

A distracting interest about other people is a trap for many, Marcus says. This is because it is not borne out of a concern for other people's welfare, but through mere curiosity. It is a great temptation because it distracts us from pursuing what is greatest and best, and is a form of time wasting. This is the life of cattle, he writes, and that the ultimate ordering of our life should be in the light of the divine.

BOOK 4

The guiding image of this book is a powerful expression of the Stoic belief in "appropriation," the idea that our intention should be to make the world our own. Our intellectual faculty, our rational part that is divine and unified, should be treated as a great fire burning at our center. Everything we encounter should be given to this fire as an advantage for itself, just as a fire consumes objects so that it can burn all the fiercer.

The self-determination we possess as rational creatures provides a retreat we can always make use of—not a physical place, like a holiday home, but somewhere even better: our own minds.

BOOK 5

Nature is a strong and consistent theme in *Meditations*. It is not enough to know our place in nature; we must actively acknowledge it by our actions. This should begin early in the day, when we are still lying in bed. As soon as we open our eyes in the morning we should face the role set out for us, as even animals and plants embrace their appointed roles in the world order.

While this is a call to action on our part, it is also an exhortation to understand the power of fate when we consider our role in the universe. Marcus gives two reasons why we should accept what fate has given us. The first is that whatever happens to you is the result of a web of fate woven specifically for you from the beginning of the world. The second is that the fated life you lead will fit perfectly into the future state of the universe. We are but one part of the universe.

BOOK 6

This book places special emphasis on the physical aspect of our mortal lives. We will be dissolved at some point to nothing but elements. This should comfort us, since we will come to properly value our soul and mind over the body. The same process can be applied to external goods. We should say to ourselves that costly Falernian wine is merely "grape juice," or that an expensive seafood dish is just "a fish's corpse." By reducing these things to their true nature, we avoid being fooled by the mere dressing of words.

The Value of Things is Deceptive

Instead of Saying:	Say:
Fish dinner	Fish corpse
Falernian wine	Grape juice
Caviar	Fish eggs
Sex	Stimulation of flesh

On a more general level, even though the physical elements are constantly changing and turning into one thing or another, we need to remember that virtue does not operate like this, and it is to the cultivation of our minds that we should turn.

BOOK 7

Change, or the specter of change, strikes fear in the hearts of many men, especially the impeding transformation of death. But everything we have seen we have already seen before, as it plays out in our own lives or on the stage of recorded world history.

Marcus makes an inventive appeal to our anxiety about the future. He says that if we bring the same care to the future, as we do in caring about the future in the present, then we have no need to worry about the future.

BOOK 8

Marcus begins this book by remarking on the fact that he can no longer spend his whole life as a philosopher, but nevertheless he can rest content in living out his life in accordance with his nature. The benefit for philosophers, as opposed to politicians, is that the former enjoy great freedom and, furthermore, have knowledge of how things really are. But, of course, this knowledge of how things are is available to everyone. When we turn our attention to do something we should focus on what is before us to see it as it truly is before we engage in that activity. Likewise, with things or animals we should seek the nature of them, determining what that nature is like when it is in a good or bad condition, and the various ways it can exist. When it comes to people, our chief concern upon meeting them should be what their relationship and attitude is toward what is good and bad.

BOOK 9

In this book, we have an examination of the various ways humans can engage in wrongdoing. Justice and lying, although they are wrongs against other human beings, turn out primarily to be impious acts against the will of the divine nature as well. Transgressions against others are transgressions against the gods, while every transgression is a transgression against the self, because in the process of doing the wrong, you make yourself worse.

BOOK 10

The trajectory of this book concerns the various relations of "parts" that we have as components of the universe. We are both a soul and a body. In so far as we are matter, we have a share in

Marcus Aurelius had political as well as philosophical obligations, but one does not need to be a philosopher to act in accordance with how things really are.

the perishable and shifting substance of the universe, but as we partake in the divine nature of rationality, we will do good to humans, who share this nature with us. We acknowledge that we share this common nature of soul and body with our fellow humans as the basis of our affection toward them. Our body and soul each require different things from us. We should fulfill these duties as long as they do not interfere with each other.

BOOK 11

Although the theme of discounting the opinions of the foolish and wicked is found throughout the *Meditations*, this is a particularly strong feature of this book. Marcus spends time speaking about our common human nature. This emphasis on reason reminds us that it is part of our rationality to recognize reason in our fellow man. He compares the alienation we experience from each other to branches severed from a tree which must be grafted back on.

There is a process we can go through to cultivate patience and sympathy with our fellow humans. Remember that some relationships will require us to be helpers, and we should note that the well-established habits of piggish and uncultivated people force them to act that way, that they act as they do from ignorance and, lastly, that oftentimes we act no differently than those we detest.

BOOK 12

This last book is a return to and repetition of common ideas seen throughout the *Meditations*. Our existence is transient and we need to acknowledge our ultimate death as a living animal. We have three parts, Marcus says: body, spirit, and mind. The body is clear enough, and there is the divine spirit, or breath, which lives within us and permeates the whole universe. The body and spirit are not truly ours, but we are their stewards. What we really own is our minds. The mind is the center of our choice and virtue, and it alone is truly ours, and it is something that we should value and perfect, both in ourselves and, insofar as we can, in the lives of others.

CHAPTER 10
Epictetus

Among all the Stoics of antiquity, Epictetus (c.AD 55–c.135) is probably the most persuasive of its advocates because of the obstacles he overcame. He lived a difficult life, beginning as the slave of a bureaucrat, Epaphroditus, in the employ of the emperor Nero. He took instruction at some point under the famous Stoic philosopher Musonius Rufus in Rome. Remarkably, he was permitted to do so while he was still enslaved. He eventually won his freedom and began teaching in Nicopolis, in Greece, after the emperor Domitian (r.AD 81–96) banned the teaching of philosophy in Rome—and later the whole of Italy—early in his reign. Nicopolis was a large coastal city founded in 29 BC by Octavian after his victory over Mark Antony at the Battle of Actium two years earlier. (It was this success that allowed Octavian to become Augustus, the first Roman emperor.) Except for occasional visits to Athens and Olympia, Epictetus remained in Nicopolis until his death. It was there that he operated, his oral teaching collected by his pupil Arrian in two great volumes, the *Discourses* and its companion the *Encheiridion*. This Greek name of the latter work translates as "in the hand" and refers to the fact that it was created as a kind of portable pocket book or handbook containing digested, edited, and reformulated sections of the *Discourses*. In the *Discourses* in particular, of

Epictetus.

which only four of the original eight books survive, there are contextual clues indicating that Epictetus in his role serving Epaphroditus was exposed to the intrigues, political jockeying, and attempts to win favor at the imperial court of Nero that serve as examples throughout the work.

The background of Epictetus provides a stark contrast to that of the two other most popular Roman Stoics, Seneca and Marcus Aurelius. He did not receive their expensive and privileged education, nor did he have set out for him an ambitious course of life through his family connections. Seneca and Epictetus did meet and make a brief acquaintance, however. And while Marcus Aurelius never met Epictetus, the latter's teachings were an influence on the *Meditations*. But in comparison to the life of ease lived by these men, Epictetus was exiled, experienced health problems, and suffered from a deformity which made him limp, and was for many years enslaved. There are reports that he gained his foot injury from a beating he received while in servitude. Whether that is true or not, his years of enslavement had a great influence on his thinking as a Stoic. They also established Epictetus's credibility as a Stoic philosopher by virtue of the fact that he had endured a difficult life outside of his choice. The principle of freedom versus enslavement is a consistent message in the *Discourses*. The enslavement that Epictetus was interested in, however, concerns that in which the mind can find itself, in service to vice and ignorance. Even an enslaved person in the court of Nero can be truly free, at least in the Stoic understanding.

THE *ENCHEIRIDION*

The words found inside the *Encheiridion*, the work on which we will chiefly concentrate, contain the oral teachings of Epictetus, a fact that should guide our reading of that text. When he spoke, Epictetus was often addressing specific questions, ideas, or even quotations in whatever way would make the Stoic position most persuasive. This is not to dismiss him. Rather, it is a reminder that we should not have the expectation when reading his spoken words that we are walking into a room to hear Stoic sermons, crafted with all the formality of an oral essay.

CHAPTER 1

This is the most important of all the lessons that Epictetus can share with us. This division will mark out what we should worry about, what we should care about, and how we should spend our time. If something is not in our power, has not been given to us to determine or decide, then we should expend no time or care on it. Keeping with his theme of enslavement as opposed to freedom, Epictetus says that the things in our power are free, while the things not in our power are slavish. The impressions that things give to us, whether a social event or the value of something bought at the store, need to be examined in light of this principle. Is this something that is under my control? If not, we should leave that thing with the dismissive truth that "it is nothing to me."

CHAPTERS 2–5

Desire is also related to whether something is in our control. If we desire something out of our control, then our desire is misplaced. To be in the right relationship to what is around us, whether a thing, a person, or a circumstance, we must take into mind the nature of a thing. For instance, we say, "I love a jug," so that when it breaks we will not be disappointed. The idea here is quite simple. By rehearsing what the nature of a thing is beforehand, we will be less surprised, shocked or dismayed by whatever can befall it. So when the ceramic jug breaks, we are already prepared by acknowledging its breakable nature.

CHAPTERS 6–9
The only thing that is ours is the use of our mind, and we should feel pride only in its proper use. If we own a beautiful horse, for example, then the beauty belongs to the horse, not us. Life is like being on a port call. You may have your fun time on the beach, but when it is time to depart and the ship of death departs, you must board.

Disease only impedes the body, but it does not hinder our moral choices, which are in our power.

CHAPTERS 10–13
For every hardship and temptation you face there is a corresponding faculty within you with which to face it. Nothing is lost, it is always "given back" and it is this we should keep in mind, even in the case of the loss of a child. Misfortunes, including any loss or theft we experience, should be considered the cost of a serene mind; the price of calmness is not free. Be content with really making progress in your soul and care not at all for how you may appear to others.

CHAPTERS 14–17

If something lies in the power of another's choice, do not spend any thought on it. Life's offerings of good and bad are like a banquet in which we should gladly partake of what is set before us, while not worrying about what is given to other guests. Do not withhold sympathetic encouragement from those in distressing conditions while recognizing that it is only their thoughts about their circumstances, not the circumstances themselves, which distress them. The gods write the play, it is up to us to perform the role assigned as best we can.

Gods write the play, we play the role.

CHAPTERS 18–21

Even if we encounter inauspicious signs, take courage that bad circumstances can benefit us. Honors and power are not under our control, so that if we recognize the nature of this "contest" we know not to even enter it. The impression of an insult is nothing but our own opinion, and distance makes this clear. If we keep the relative misfortunes of death and exile ever before us, then you will never have any lowly thoughts.

CHAPTERS 22–25

If you desire to be a philosopher, you must accept the scorn of others. Anyone who caters to the wishes of what others want will lose a solid standing in life. Do not compromise yourself for the benefit of society, for then what is the value of society with people such as yourself in it? If someone besides yourself has been honored, if it is a rightly bestowed honor, then rejoice; if unjustly conferred, be glad that you do not have such poor judgment.

CHAPTERS 26–29

Be consistent in your application of the difficulties of mortal nature to yourself. If you offer a consolation to others, then use that same consolation in your case; you are not exempt. Evil is analogous to completely missing the mark of a target, so we should acknowledge that evil is not natural. We would get very distressed if someone handed over our body to another; how much more should we protect our mind, when it is "handed over" to another when he curses or reviles us? Consider both the beginning and the end of any project, so that you do not give up the task when difficulties arise.

CHAPTERS 30–33

Our duties to our fellow man are determined by the relationships we have to them, such as father to son, or daughter to mother. The most important element of our piety to the gods is that, since they administer the universe, we ought to submit to their providence in whatever we experience in life. What is destined to occur cannot affect what is in our control, our choice of good over evil. We ought to avoid talking when possible, and when we do, not to talk about other people.

CHAPTERS 34–37

When entertaining the possibility of a pleasure, wait a while before taking it up and consider beforehand what it will amount to both during and after. Be proud to do anything which you have determined must be done. Show proper respect on social occasions. Never take on roles which you cannot perform, for you disgrace yourself by incompetency and by neglecting your true role.

CHAPTERS 38–41

As one is careful to guard one's feet from physical dangers, we should watch what we focus our mind upon. The proper limitation on our property is only what is necessary to supply the needs of the body. We should spend comparatively little time, and only so much as is necessary, on the cultivation of the body. We should focus instead on the mind.

CHAPTERS 42–45

Anytime we are mistreated we should turn to the thought that the person so behaving is working off a deception of judgment, that "it seems so to him." Each situation has two "handles" by which we can approach it, a good perspective and a bad perspective. Having property or more skill than someone does not make a person superior, it only means they have more property or skill. Reserve judgments when claiming someone does something "poorly" or "badly."

CHAPTERS 46–49

Do not take the name philosopher nor even offer up to others your philosophical beliefs, but let them be demonstrated by your way of life. When you have adjusted yourself to the simple life of austerity, do not let others see or know this. The philosophical mind ought to expect all good or bad to come from itself and no other. If you are pretentious in the reading of texts, then you have nothing to boast about, for that accomplishment was the work of another, the author.

CHAPTERS 50–52

Sticking by your principles is under your control, while the opinions of others about how you stick to your principles is not under your control. Do not delay in enacting the life of virtue that you are already informed about, as there is no teacher who can teach you what you already know. The application of an ethical principle is more important than the arguments which justify it.

CHAPTER 53

This last chapter of the *Encheiridion* focuses on two main ideas. The first is that we should depend on the providence of the gods; the second is to remember that we cannot be injured by wicked men. What is in our control is our virtue, which we take with us in life until our death.

CHAPTER 11

Impression

The concept of an impression is a very technical term, forming the basis for the entire Stoic theory of knowledge. It is often rendered as impression, representation, or appearance. The Greek word is *phantasia*, from which the English word "fantasy" is derived. It is a word linked to appearance and shares a common root with the Greek word *phenomenon*.

The impression, or the idea of an impression, is clearly taken first of all from sight. An impression, understood as an appearance, must appear in some way to us, and that appearing is either visual or plays off the metaphor of the visual. Think of how we say "I see" when an idea makes sense to us, or, when responding to a proposal we ask the person to "show it to me," when what is under consideration cannot, in fact, be seen or shown to any physical eyes.

THE TWO PARTS OF AN IMPRESSION AND PHANTASMA

The two parts of an impression are linked together, in the philosophical process they are describing and etymologically. The two parts are impression (*phantasia*) and impressor (*phantaston*). A figment (*phantasma*) and imagination (*phantastikon*) are related concepts, but they are distinct from the impression process.

THE IMPRESSOR

It is easiest to start with the impressor. This is the object or thing which will set off an impression in us. In simple cases, this is anything which is capable of being perceived by the normal sense faculties of a human being. Anything with color, taste, sound, touch, or smell is an impressor. A white flower, for example, is an impressor.

THE IMPRESSION

The corresponding half to the impressor is the impression itself. If the impressor is something external, then the impression is that internal effect that takes place in the soul. When we talk about an impression, it cannot be separated from the impressor. The reason is that the impression is a necessary and faithful effect of the impressor. Using the white flower example, what we say is the flower, as impressor, gives us the impression of something white, with petals and so forth. The impression, in other words, is an indicator of the nature of what gives rise to it.

IMPRESSOR AND IMPRESSION

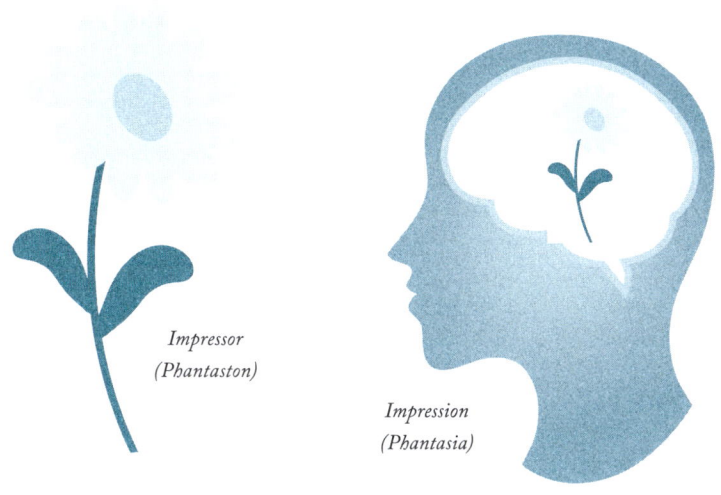

Impressor (Phantaston)

Impression (Phantasia)

IMAGINATION

An instance of imagination is somewhat like an impression, in that it is the form of an image being presented to the mind. However, the crucial distinction is that imagination does not arise from an impressor but is entirely a fabrication of a person's mind.

FIGMENT

A figment is a kind of imagination that apparently arises when there is some kind of illness or other disordering of a human's organism, so that its illusory nature once again comes about through something that is not an impressor.

THE ROLE OF THE MIND

Given that there is something external, an impressor, of whatever kind it is, and there is the impression, occurring within the mind, the role of thinking plays a large part in the formation of impressions. A number of distinctions are made within the mind when an impression is given. One is that the impressor exists as some determinate object out there in the world. We can say "this flower is white," or "that woman is by the car." In other words, the impression informs us about the impressor.

CHOICE IN IMPRESSIONS

At first, the impression is merely an impression, presenting itself in a certain way to the mind. It has no magical powers of its own to convince us of its veracity. The Stoic emphasis on choice is prominent in this area of the philosophy. An impression is formed in our mind of the way something appears, but that does not mean we have to assent to that impression. It has to be granted, and this permission, so to speak, to subject oneself to what the impression appears as, is a very important task in our daily life. The ultimate decision as to whether or not we accept an impression does not reside in the sense organs, but in the mind itself. It is a choice to accept the impression as it is, or not.

LANGUAGE AND LEVELS

The process that began with the impression continues with an increasing level of complexity. Once an impression is accepted by us, we then assign a number of linguistic or proto-linguistic descriptions, such as "that is a cat," or "that moving black thing is a cat." The level of classification enlarges with experience. As we gain more impressions we begin to form categories, such as animal, or mortal, and so forth. The lower levels of experience contribute to the formation of these higher levels through memory.

SENSES AND IMPRESSIONS

As we have seen, the impressions are explained through the usually clear case of sense perception. This does not mean that an impression always has to result from something strictly perceptual. Rather, the Stoic reliance on the senses to explain their theory of knowledge shows two things. One is that this theory of impressions is one that all humans experience. The Stoics are not claiming that other people think in a different way and that their theory is the true and best way to think. Everyone is already thinking in this way, it is just a question of how well we are making use of our mental faculties, the "ruling part" as the Stoics say. The second reason for this appeal to sense perception is that, although not all impressions occur through the physical senses, they occur in a similar manner. That is, all other impressions take place in an analogous manner to the way in which sense perceptions do. "The man appears to be just," is, in principle, an impression just as much as "The man appears to be tanned," even though being just is not visible in the same way that being tanned is.

THE COGNITIVE IMPRESSION

So far, we have discussed the way in which the Stoics understand the mind to work. An impression is given to us and we are to decide whether that impression is true or not. The impression has a certain kind of character in the case that it is true and should be accepted. This kind of true impression gains the name "cognitive impression." It is a cognitive impression and only a cognitive impression if it gives a true presentation of the object from which it comes.

This idea of the cognitive impression plays an essential role in the Stoic theory of knowledge. With this commitment the Stoics have an empirically based justification for how to come to knowledge. The language they use emphasizes the tight relationship between impressor and impression, or the object giving rise to the impression and the impression itself. In the case of a cognitive impression, they compared the process to that of a wax stamp. In that case, by looking at the seal created by the stamp, we know the nature of the stamp as well. They cannot be separated because the seal, standing in for the impression, bears the marks and character of the stamp, or external object, which gave rise to it.

THE CHARACTERISTIC MARK OF THE COGNITIVE IMPRESSION

Not everyone was in agreement with the innovation of the Stoics when it came to cognitive impressions. The objection boiled down to one point in particular. Can a false impression be just like a cognitive impression? The Stoic position was that this is impossible, but they were pushed to defend this point. The route they took was to say that there is some character of a cognitive impression which makes it necessarily distinct from what is a false impression. They altered their definition of a cognitive impression to the qualification that a cognitive impression has to arise in a way that it could not arise from what is not. By this they meant that the cognitive impression has a direct relationship to, and is therefore a direct reflection of, something that exists. If there is something that exists out there, then our cognitive impression of it is an indication not only that it does exist, but that the impression of it is true.

FALSE AND TRUE IMPRESSIONS

Another form of objection the Stoics faced in their advocacy for impressions concerns the hard cases where it is difficult to discern what is true and false. For instance, the Stoic Sphaerus was invited to Ptolemy's court in Alexandria. While there he was shown pomegranates and, in the process, perhaps by attempting to peel and eat one of the fruits, he discovered that the pomegranate was made of wax. The king had purposely attempted to deceive him and pointed out the mistake. But Sphaerus denied that he gave his assent that they were pomegranates. What he said was that he gave his assent to the impression that it was reasonable to think that they were pomegranates. So, the fake pomegranates gave off the *reasonable* impression that they were pomegranates, but real pomegranates would give the *cognitive* impression that they were truly pomegranates—and only real pomegranates are capable of the true or cognitive impression.

WITHHOLDING ASSENT FROM AN IMPRESSION

The precise nature and, indeed, even the existence of cognitive impressions was a point of dispute with others who were opposed to the Stoic theory of knowledge. Chief among these were the heirs of Plato's Academy. But there was no doubt on either side of this debate that there could be false or illusory impressions. From the Stoic perspective, for example, we see the remains of a slender tree sticking up through a pool of fresh water. We notice that through the water the stick appears to be bent. But we withhold our assent to this impression because we know that the water is altering the appearance of the stick in the water. We do not come to believe that the stick is bent, because we know that something funny is going on, and we refuse to believe for this very reason. Notice too that we are not compelled to believe that the stick is perfectly straight. Our knowledge of the distortion of the water is enough for us to withhold assent.

A further example is a person standing at some distance from me. He looks no bigger than my hand, and this is the impression that my eyes deliver to me. But I am not obliged to assent to this impression. This would be a mistake, however, as I am familiar with the differences in distances and how this changes my visual perception of something. Once again, I withhold my assent from this particular impression—I am justified in not believing the man is three feet (one metre) tall.

These examples give us some insight into what is occurring with impressions in general and cognitive impressions in particular. It is the distinctive mark of a wise man to never give his assent to an impression which is not cognitive. These examples show us that experience and scrutiny are both conditions that should be applied at all times to every impression. When an impression, of any kind, presents itself to us our default should not be to just accept what we are given. Assent has to be earned; knowledge must be worked for.

COGNITIVE IMPRESSIONS COMPARED

With these examples of non-cognitive impressions in mind, let us consider again the cognitive impression by contrast. The cognitive impression has a special character to it. When some external object or thing is encountered by a normal human being, it triggers an impression matching the character of the external object. There is nothing beyond this experience of the cognitive impression to which we can appeal as a confirmation of the truth of the impression. The impression itself carries this nature along with it. This is ultimately why the Stoics consider the cognitive impression "the criterion of truth." Everything in our experience is built upon this foundation, and such impressions are verified by having them, and everything in our language and thought follows from these impressions and their truth.

CHAPTER 12
Neo-Stoicism

Neo-Stoicism is the name given to the modern revival of Stoicism that emerged around the turn of the new millennium. It is a revival but it is also an adaptation. This is mainly because, of the three branches of Stoicism, only ethics is viewed as of modern relevance. Physics and logic are pushed off to the side as impractical or outdated. In a way, this is completely understandable. The most popular exponents of Stoicism, Seneca, Epictetus and Marcus Aurelius, were all focused on ethical life in their writings and touched on logic and physics only lightly.

Neo-Stoicism often takes on the appearance of a self-help movement, since it focuses on self-improvement. From the very beginning of Stoicism there has been a tension between the providence established in the world through Zeus as a vitalizing spirit and the extreme emphasis placed on the cultivation of the self.

This focus on virtue emphasizes personal agency and accountability, and this is one of the hallmarks of modern Neo-Stoicism.

The Neo-Stoic emphasis begins in the same place as Epictetus, between the division of all our experiences into things we can control and things we cannot. It is, above all, a movement geared toward self-improvement and self-control in the service of becoming the best person we can be. There is more than just a hint that modern approaches have failed us, that the therapy of technology, modern psychological appeals to drugs, and the general social changes we have seen in the twenty-first century have fundamentally disrupted the way humans live. One advantage of turning to the Stoics is that their philosophy is time tested. The Stoic position was hashed out through many centuries of the rough experience of human history and has been put into practice through hundreds of thousands of lives. There is also the assumption that human nature has not changed, that the ethical and mental life problems we face today are fundamentally of a similar character to those faced by Epictetus and Zeno.

Stoicism has gained such prominence that there are multiple so-called "Stoicons" each year. At these Stoic conferences professional philosophers as well as laypeople interested in progressing in Stoicism get together to pursue the philosophy's tenets. They take place within the context of a Stoic week, with different days devoted to different topics, such as "mindfulness," "virtue," or "relationships."

A striking instance of the practical vitality found in Stoicism, and one of the defining episodes for its emergence as a subject of modern interest, was the rise to public prominence in the US of

Admiral James Stockdale as a political candidate for high office. This took place in 1992, when the businessman and philanthropist Ross Perot put himself forward as a third party candidate in the US presidential election against the Republican George H. W. Bush and the Democrat Bill Clinton and chose Stockdale as his vice-presidential running mate. In interviews and profiles regarding his candidature, Stockdale spoke openly about his belief in Stoicism, which he credited with helping him to cope with his time as a captive during the Vietnam War.

Stockdale said that he told himself, as he was descending in a parachute after being shot out of his A-4 Skyhawk attack aircraft: "Five years down there at least. I'm leaving the world of technology and entering the world of Epictetus."

It turned out to be three years instead of five, but he was brutally tortured and chained to a bathtub during his time as a prisoner of war. As this happened, he remembered the philosophical admonitions of Epictetus to focus on what was under his control, which Stockdale took to be that what is "within my will, are my opinions, my attitude toward what is going on, my own good, and my own evil."

The courageous and inspiring history of Stockdale was one of the seminal moments in the modern appreciation for Stoicism. It was followed in 1998 by the publication of two influential books that publicized the philosophy further. *The Inner Citadel* was a new translation of Marcus Aurelius's *Meditations* in which the philosopher Pierre Hadot also included an insightful commentary and penetrating analysis of the Roman emperor's work. *The New Stoicism* by Lawrence Becker, meanwhile, was intended as a manifesto for an updated and adapted form of Stoicism. In his book, Becker looked at how the Stoicism of centuries past had been robbed and appropriated for religious purposes. He then addressed the issue of how scientific and technological developments have rendered certain Stoic tenets redundant, such as the belief that the god Zeus permeates all matter. In Becker's recasting of the philosophy, he urged its adherents to focus their beliefs on nature rather than look for any great cosmic purpose, as is the case with classical Stoicism, whose Zeus and fate provided the universe with a design and a goal.

The Obstacle is the Way, published in 2014, is, according to its author Ryan Holiday, "ruthlessly practical." The main conceit of the book is to take whatever bad things we encounter in life and see how we can transform them to our benefit. The idea is not to turn bugs into butterflies but lemons into lemonade. There are opportunities hiding in everything that we view as negative. The book does not go deep and proudly simplifies. It is punchy and helpful, filled with anecdotes of modern examples of perseverance.

Central to the modern Stoic revival has been its association with and similarities to modern psychological theories. One of these, Cognitive Behavioral Therapy (CBT), while not aimed specifically at the elimination of emotions, which is a key Stoic objective, does seek to free those who undergo it from destructive feelings by investigating underlying beliefs of behavior. Once the beliefs are identified they can be targeted so that new beliefs can supplant them or adapt them as necessary. Although this approach is not explicitly inspired by Stoicism, it should be taken as a partial independent confirmation of the success that can be had when applying Stoic ideas to life.

There are two general areas in which CBT can be applied: thoughts and behavior. Both, of course, are things that are under our control, to put it into Stoic language. The remediation of these faulty or destructive ways of thinking and acting centers on examining the self. When the sources of these beliefs and actions have been properly identified they can be compared to reality, and alternative and better options can be chosen. Donald Robertson, a popular modern exponent of Stoicism, presents himself as a "cognitive-behavioral psychotherapist."

THEMES IN NEO-STOICISM
SELF-MASTERY
Neo-Stoicism emphasizes the control we have over our own lives, especially as it relates to our emotional life.

VICTORY
This is an unexpected aim of any attempt to resuscitate Stoicism, since virtue alone is the main and arguably only goal of ancient Stoicism. Neo-Stoicism in this formulation is promoted as a path of discipline into various accomplishments, personal and professional.

PEACE
With today's world of hustle and bustle, and the confusing omnipresence of social and news media, the modern person

is often in search of respite, some way in which to escape and recharge. Stoicism offers up an opportunity for such escape, in the refuge of the inner self. The self-reflection involved in the Stoic life delivers a level of peace and serenity. The search for peace is a turn away from stress and the burdens of modern life.

SHORT AND UNDERSTANDABLE

One distinct advantage that Stoicism has as a movement is that it is straightforward and pithy. This is especially true in the case of Marcus Aurelius and Epictetus, whose sayings are mostly broken up into small, digestible sections. But the content is quite simple as well, if we compare it to the often perplexing writings of Plato and Aristotle, for example.

PROGRESS

This is a tremendously underappreciated aspect of Stoicism's appeal. From the very beginning, the Stoics were emphatic that only the perfectly wise man was virtuous. But despite this lofty ideal, they were equally clear that all other Stoics were "progressors." Making progress through the meticulous discipline of self-improvement, and marking these improvements, is central to Stoicism.

REGULARITY AND RULES

While it is not fair to Stoicism to reduce it to a set of rules, it certainly is possible to distill the heart of much of its ethical teaching into memorable and impactful statements. The practical elements of Stoicism can be readily understood and applied. This also explains why there are Stoic "bibles," notebooks, and meditative calendars filled with quotations. The nature of Stoicism lends itself to regular and disciplined daily reminders of its key insights.

MASCULINITY

It would be hard to deny that the appeal, and even the purpose, of much Neo-Stoic material is directed at men. The popular connotations of the word "stoic" no doubt contribute to this, but so too do the traditionally masculine associated aims of success and overcoming the self.

RELIGIOUS ALTERNATIVE

Another appeal of Stoicism is that it is bereft of traditional religious teachings. This, of course, only applies to the modern version of Stoicism, which has done away with Zeus and other aspects of the divine. This secular vantage point gives an alternative for those seeking something other than religion, though it still provides some of the advantages of religious adherence.

ORDER AND DISCIPLINE

Stoicism is impossible to take on without a commitment to discipline. It challenges the individual to focus on the cultivation of daily habits and the elimination of harmful beliefs and actions.

VERSATILITY

Stoicism is a belief system that can live comfortably alongside a number of other views and beliefs about mankind. So not only can Stoicism apply to personal life, but it also increasingly pops up in business circles. Because it is not viewed as a religious conviction, Stoicism is not a threat nor an illicit insertion of religious belief into the workplace.

INDIVIDUALISM

This feature of Stoicism is a selling point, though, of course, it could also be seen as a drawback. But since Stoicism focuses on what "I can do," in direct and explicit contrast to what others do, it is only natural that Stoicism attracts those who can improve themselves without any appeal to the judgment or companionship of others.

In summary, there are many practical and attractive features of Stoicism that can be applied to modern circumstances. There is a thriving industry of different efforts claiming to adapt or otherwise make more accessible the works of ancient Stoics. In fact, it is reasonable to suppose that many of these authors, books, and conventions have built upon the foundation of Stoicism, contributing new insights into the old system and new methods of studying it. Stoicism does have much it can say to us, if we are willing to open up a dialogue with the Stoics themselves.

INDEX

Academy 8–9, 16, 17, 37, 186
accomplishments 198
Agora 8, 9, 18
air as element 69–72
Antoninus Pius, Emperor 147
Apocolocyntosis (Seneca) 131–2
appearances and passion 87–8
appropriation 119–22, 149–50
Aristotle 8, 17, 39, 40–1, 68
Arrian 160
Athens 8–9
Attalos 129
Augustus, Emperor 160
Balbus 101–2, 104–5
Becker, Lawrence 195–6
blending in nature 74–5
Caesar, Julius 128
Caligula, Emperor 129–30
Cato 122
Chrysippus 31
   argumentation 38
   on blending in nature 74, 75
   disputes with Cleanthes 35–6
   on elements 71
   on Ethics 42–5
   founder of Stoicism 34–5
   on Logic 39
   on passions 86
   on Physics 41–2, 43
   on providential interconnectedness 108–9
   resistance to 37–8
   on the Soul 39, 40–1
   at Stoa 10
Cicero 95, 101–2, 122
Claudius, Emperor 130, 132
Cleanthes 35
   disputes with Chrysippus 35–6
   and the gods 104
   at Stoa 32–4
   founder of Stoicism 10
Cognitive Behavioral Therapy (CBT) 197–8
cognitive impression 182–5, 186–9
composition of the Soul 72–4
Crates 17
death 135–8
Determinism 58–61
Diognetus 147
Discourses (Epictetus) 37, 49–50, 160–1
Domitia Calvilla 144
Domitian, Emperor 160
elements 68–72, 96–8
emotions see passions
Encheiridion (Epictetus) 11, 160–1, 162–73, 175
Epictetus
   and Chrysippus 37
   and *Discourses* 37, 49–50, 160–1
   and *Encheiridion* 11, 160–1, 162–73, 175
   on impressions 187
   life of 160–2
   on nature 63, 67
   and Neo-Stoicism 199
   on passions 89
   popularizer of Stoicism 10–11
   on virtue 49–50, 53
Epicureanism 8, 29, 44–5
Epicurus 8, 28, 138
eternal recurrence 75–7, 101
Ethics
   Chrysippus on 42–5
   as division of Stoic philosophy 20–2, 27
eudaimonia 43–4
eupatheiai 93
fate 76–7
fire
   as element 68–72
   and eternal recurrence 75–7
   in design of the universe 96–9
free will 58–61
Gallio, Junius 128
gods
   Cicero on 95, 101–2
   and design of the universe 96–101
   and intelligence of the universe 106–7
   and politics 122–3
   providential interconnectedness 108–9
   Stoical belief in 101–6
Hadot, Pierre 195
Hadrian, Emperor 144
happiness
   in Ethics 43–4
   and Virtue 53–4
hegemonikon 40, 41
Hierocles 119–20
Holiday, Ryan 196–7
imagination 178–80
impressions
   choices in 181
   and cognitive impression 182–5, 186–9
   description of 176
   dispute over 35–6
   Epictetus on 187
   false and true 185–6
   and impression 176, 178
   and impressor 176–7
   and imagination 178–80
   language of 181
   levels of 181
   mind in 180
   senses in 182
individuals
   fulfilment of nature of

116–18
and Neo-Stoicism
  201–2
and relationships
  118–22
self-preservation 114–16
inner peace 199
Laertius, Diogenes 31,
  180
Letters from a Stoic
  (Seneca) 116, 117, 136
*Lives and Opinions of
  Eminent Philosophers,
  The* (Laertius) 31, 180
Logic
  Chrysippus on 39
  as division of Stoic
    philosophy 20–2, 27–9
Lucan 128
Lyceum 8, 17
Marcus Annius Varus 144
Marcus Aurelius 7
  and Epictetus 161–2
  life of 144–7
  and *Meditations* 7, 47,
    79, 143, 144, 147–57,
    162, 191, 195
  and Neo-Stoicism 199
  on nature 151–2
  on passions 79
  popularizer of
    Stoicism 10–11
  on virtue 47
Marcus Cornelius Fronto
  147
masculinity 200
Meditations (Marcus
  Aurelius) 7, 47, 79,
  143, 144, 147–57, 162,
  191, 195
Megarian school 17
mind in impressions 180
mixture in nature 74–5
Musonius Rufus 160
natural law 123–5
nature
  blending and mixture
    74–5
  composition of the
    Soul 72–4

and design of the
  universe 96–101
elements in 68–72,
  96–8
Epictetus on 63, 67
eternal recurrence
  75–7, 101
mankind's place in
  65–7
Marcus Aurelius on
  151–2
ontology of 64–5
providential intercon-
  nectedness 108–9
Neo-Stoicism
  and Cognitive
    Behavioral Therapy
    (CBT) 197–8
  description of 192–8
  themes in 198–202
Nero, Emperor 130, 131
Nerva, Emperor 144
New Stoicism, The (Becker)
  195
Obstacle is the Way, The
  (Holiday) 196–7
On Anger (Seneca) 87, 88
On the Brevity of Life
  (Seneca) 134
On Ends (Cicero) 122
On the Nature of the Gods
  (Cicero) 95, 101–2
On the Word (Zeno) 20
Oracle at Delphi 16
Painted Porch 8, 9–10,
  17–18
passions
  and appearances 87–8
  Chrysippus on 86
  division of 81–2, 83
  elimination of 89–92
  Epictetus on 89
  and *eupatheiai* 93
  Marcus Aurelius on
    79
  material nature of 84–6
  nature of 80–1
  and reason 88
  as a tyrant 86–7
  and virtue 82–3, 90–2

Paul, St 128
Peripatetic school 17
Perot, Ross 194
Physics
  Chrysippus on 41–2,
    43
  as division of Stoic philos-
    ophy 20–6
Piso, Gaius Calpurnius
  130
Plato 8, 16, 17, 37, 39,
  40–1, 68, 114, 186
Polemo 16, 20
politics
  and gods 122–3
  and natural law 123–5
Zeno on 111, 112–14
Pompey the Great 128
prokoptōn 56
providential interconnectedness 108–9
Pythagoreanism 129
reason 88
regularity in Neo–
  Stoicism 200
relationships 118–22
Republic (Plato) 114
Republic (Zeno) 112
Robertson, Donald 198
sages 54–7
sayables 23, 24, 25–6, 28
secularism 200–1
self-discipline 201
self-improvement
  199–200
self-mastery 198
Seneca 45, 127
  on death 135–8
  on fulfilment of
    nature 116, 117
  life of 128–31
  on passions 87, 88
  popularizer of
    Stoicism 10–11
  on use of time 133–5
  on virtue 138–41
  writings of 131–2
Seneca the Elder 128
senses 182
Sextius, Quintus 129

Socrates 16–17
Soul
  Chrysippus on 39, 40–1
  composition of 72–4
  and virtue 51–2
Sphaerus 185–6
Stilpo 16
Stoa 9–10, 17–18, 32, 34–5
Stockdale, James 194–5
Stoicism
  disagreements with other philosophical schools 8–10
  division into Ethics, Logic, and Physics 20–9
  founded 8, 10, 16–17
  as practical philosophy 10
time, use of 133–5
Trajan, Emperor 144

tree of flutes 106–7
unity of mind 51–3
versatility 201
vice 57–8
virtue
  and Determinism 58–61
  Epictetus on 49–50, 53
  and free will 58–61
  and happiness 53–4
  importance of 48–9, 50
  nature of 50–1
Marcus Aurelius on 47
and passions 82–3, 90–2
and sages 54–7
Seneca on 138–41
and the Soul 51–2
and unity of mind 51–3
and vice 57–8
Xenocrates 16
Xenophon 16

Zeno of Citium 15
  and Cleanthes 32
  and divisions of Stoic philosophy 22, 27, 28
  framework of Stoicism 29
  founder of Stoicism 8, 10, 16–17
  importance in Stoicism 11, 36–7
  on intelligence of the universe 106–7
  originality of 19–20
  on politics 111, 112–14
  on the Soul 74
  at Stoa 18–19
  on virtue 48
Zeus 96–7, 98, 99–101, 106, 196

PICTURE CREDITS

Adobe Stock: 6, 46, 63, 64, 84

Shutterstock: 11, 16, 20, 22, 35, 40, 41, 49, 68, 69, 82, 97, 100, 104, 111

Wellcome Collection: 55

Wikimedia Commons: 8, 25, 26